THE ALLEGED BUDGET SURPLUS,

SOCIAL SECURITY,

&

VOODOO ECONOMICS

Allen W. Smith, Ph.D.
Author of
Demystifying Economics

IRONWOOD PUBLICATIONS
Naples, Florida

Library of Congress Card Number 00-191559

ISBN 0-9648504-5-1

Printed in the United States of America

For my wife,
Joan Rugel Smith

and

my children,
Mark, Michael, and Lisa

CONTENTS

PREFACE

When I first began using credit cards many years ago, my young children seemed to think that those tiny pieces of plastic represented some kind of magic. They watched me buy merchandise without paying for it, and as far as they could see, I never paid for anything. They were too young to understand that for every dollar I charged to the credit cards, I became one dollar deeper in debt.

Some naïve adults seem to also think of credit cards as magic. They lack the self-discipline to keep their spending within the bounds of their income. The "buy now and pay later" message of merchants comes across loud and clear. As long as they have not exceeded the credit limits on their cards, they just continue to buy whatever they want as if there were no limit to how much they could spend. But there is a limit, and such people eventually end up in bankruptcy court unless they learn to mend their ways before it is too late.

For the past twenty years, the United States government has been behaving like an irresponsible and immature person with an unlimited supply of credit. During that period, the national debt rose from $1 trillion to more than $5.6 trillion. Considering the fact that it took this nation more than 200 years—from the nation's birth until 1981—to accumulate the first trillion dollars of debt, it was disturbing to watch our government accumulate the second trillion dollars of debt in just five years. How could a nation add as much to its national debt in just five years as it had accumulated during the previous 200 years? The answer, of course, was that the nation was spending billions of dollars more than it was collecting in tax revenue each and every year. In 1986, the year that the debt passed the $2 trillion mark, the government ran an on-budget deficit of $238.0 billion. Any household or business firm would have been forced to put its house in order after exhibiting such reckless fiscal behavior, but not the United States Government. The federal government continued to pay for today's government with tomorrow's money year after year for nearly two decades. The nation was drowning in red ink.

The restoration of some of the lost revenue from the Reagan tax cuts, in the form of the tax increase at the beginning of the Clinton Administration, finally resulted in enough revenue to provide a tiny $0.7 billion on-budget (excluding Social Security) surplus in 1999, a year in which the unemployment rate was at a 30-year low. But there was not enough revenue (excluding Social Security) to avoid on-budget deficits in years when the unemployment rate was higher, or to pay back the debt accumulated in previous years.

Just since 1981, the government has borrowed more than $4.6 trillion ($4,600 billion or $4,600,000 million) to cover its deficit spending. We still owe all that money plus the $1 trillion in debt that was accumulated prior to 1981, and the interest on the debt is costing American taxpayers more than $350 billion per year!

CHAPTER 1

INTRODUCTION

Probably never before in American history have the citizens been so misled by so many people on an issue of such great importance to their future and the future of the nation. Our two-party system usually guarantees that when the leaders of one party try to put something over on the voters, the other party cries foul. In addition, the news media have been very diligent in the past to point out the errors of political leaders to the electorate. But a unique set of circumstances has led to what appears to be one of the greatest misrepresentations ever perpetrated on the American people.

There is a gross misunderstanding on the part of most Americans as to the financial condition of the United States Government. Even worse, this misunderstanding has the potential to lead to actions that could inflict serious damage on the booming American economy.

Most people seem to be under the mistaken notion that our government's financial position has improved so much that the government now has excess money to spend on new programs and/or to finance a major tax cut. Nothing could be farther from the truth. In terms of indebtedness, the federal government's financial condition is worse today than ever before in the history of the nation.

There is no mystery as to where the public got the idea that the government has somehow stumbled onto a gigantic windfall of excess money. They have been told this over and over by President Clinton and by both presidential candidates. George W. Bush has even promised a $1.3 trillion reduction in income taxes over the next 10 years, citing the alleged surplus as his source for funding the large tax cut. Given the fact that the government has more than $4.5 trillion in unpaid bills just from its spending over the past 20 years, the idea of reducing the nation's revenue by an additional $1.3 trillion without corresponding cuts in spending is preposterous.

Why would President Clinton, Al Gore, George W. Bush, and a host of other politicians from both parties deliberately mislead the American people on such a crucial matter? The only plausible explanation is that they are trying to convince the people that a surplus exists because the surplus myth fits well into their political agenda.

President Clinton and Vice President Gore want a budget surplus to exist so they can claim that the Clinton Administration, which inherited massive budget deficits, eliminated the deficits and transformed them into large surpluses in just eight years. George W. Bush wants a surplus to exist so that he can promise major tax cuts and attempt to get to the White House riding the same horse that carried Ronald Reagan to the Oval Office.

The existence of a real budget surplus is in the best interests of both political parties, and the voters love the idea that the government has become so rich that it can give money back to the people. It is like believing in Santa Claus. All parties have such a strong desire for a real surplus to exist that they pretend that such a surplus actually does exist. But there is no "real" budget surplus in any meaningful sense of the term!

In order to have any credibility, these people must have a way to "prove" that there is a budget surplus. So they take the annual total dollar inflow of funds to the federal government, including the Social Security tax revenue, and subtract from that number the annual total dollar outflow of funds, including the benefits that Social Security is currently paying out. The net result from this calculation shows that the total receipts flowing into the federal government exceed the total expenditures flowing out by a substantial amount at the present time. Thus, politicians use this calculation to "prove"'" that there is a surplus in the federal budget. Technically, they are correct on this point, but they fail to tell the rest of the story. All of the surplus belongs to the Social Security Trust Fund.

Funds flowing into and out of the Social Security Trust Fund are by law supposed to be kept separate from other government expenditures. So the government has a real surplus only if its total spending for everything, except Social Security benefits, is less than its total revenue from all sources except Social Security taxes. Such a surplus has not existed in a single year since 1960 with the possible exception of fiscal year 1999. The Treasury Department initially reported a deficit of $1 billion for 1999. However, the numbers were later revised, and a tiny $0.7 billion surplus was reported. The numbers are so close that the most we can say is that the budget was approximately balanced in 1999 for the first time in 39 years.

The approximately balanced budget for 1999 occurred at a time when the unemployment rate was at a 30-year low and corporate profits were soaring. Since almost all of the federal government's revenue (excluding Social Security contributions) comes from individual income taxes and corporation income taxes, there should have been a much larger surplus in a year when the economy was so overheated. Most economists believe that there should be budget surpluses in those years when the economy is operating at full employment to offset the deficits that occur when it is operating below the full-employment level. If the tax structure was not sufficient to bring a balanced budget at any time other than during such an extraordinarily prosperous year as fiscal 1999, then we are likely to return to deficits at the first hint of rising unemployment. Why would anybody suggest additional cuts in tax rates under these circumstances and make continuing large budget deficits almost a certainty over the long run?

The federal government ran a deficit in its operating budget each and every year from 1961 through 1998. In 1999, the operating budget was approximately balanced for the first time in 39 years with a possible tiny surplus of $0.7 billion. That's it! That is the whole surplus in the government's operating budget! During the previous four years, 1995-98, the government ran deficits totaling $534 billion. A possible $0.7 billion surplus in 1999 doesn't do a great deal to offset all the red ink of previous years.

The Social Security Trust Fund does have a planned surplus at this time. A Presidential Commission headed by Alan Greenspan recommended in 1982 that payroll taxes be increased in order to partially pre-fund the retirement of the baby boomers, the largest generation in American history.

In 1983, legislation was enacted to improve the solvency of the Social Security Trust Fund which ran small budget deficits for seven years in a row from 1976-1982. The legislation was designed specifically for the purpose of building up a surplus in the Trust Fund in preparation for the staggering new obligations the Fund would face when the baby-boom generation begins to retire about 2010. Both Social Security tax rates and the Social Security tax base were gradually raised over a seven-year period so the Trust Fund would be solvent when it took the big financial hit resulting from the retirement of the baby boomers. Specifically, the legislation gradually raised the Social Security tax rate from 6.7 percent in 1983 to 7.65 percent in 1990, and raised the tax base from $35,700 in 1983 to $51,300 in 1990.

The game plan worked. By 1986, the off-budget surplus of the federal government, which is made up mostly of the Social Security surplus, had risen to $16.7 billion.

The Social Security surplus was $52.8 billion in 1989, and it had soared to $123.7 billion in 1999. This planned surplus in the Social Security Trust Fund will be wiped out over the next several years by increased Social Security payouts to the baby boomers, and the Trust Fund is expected to begin experiencing deficits again beginning about 2015. Yet, politicians can't keep their eye off that temporary surplus in the Social Security cookie jar and are making plans to use it in various ways, including giving part of it to higher-income Americans in the form of a tax cut.

Actually, the government has been borrowing the Social Security surplus and spending it on general government programs for several years. The net effect has been to disguise the true size of budget deficits in past years. For example, in fiscal year 1995, the government experienced a $226.4 billion deficit in its operating budget. However, since the Social Security Trust Fund had a surplus of $62.4 billion that year, the government simply borrowed the Social Security surplus and spent it as part of it general operating budget. The $62.4 billion Social Security surplus was deducted from the $226.4 billion deficit and the government reported an official deficit of only $164 billion.

In 1997, since there was a surplus in the Social Security Trust Fund of $81.4 billion, the actual $103.4 billion on-budget deficit was reduced by that amount and the government reported a total deficit of only $22.0 billion. It was in 1998 that the American people first had the wool pulled over their eyes on a grand scale. In that year, the operating budget of the federal government was still in the red with an actual deficit of $30 billion. It was the $99.2 billion surplus in the Social Security Trust Fund that enabled the government to report a budget surplus of $69.2 billion. During a year in which the United States Government spent $30 billion more than it collected in general revenue, it announced that there was a $69.2 billion overall surplus!

From that point on, the American people seemed to believe that there truly was excess money in the federal budget, and cunning politicians began building schemes to further mislead the people into believing that money was available for new programs and/or for cutting taxes. Any reader who has doubts about whether the government had a deficit or surplus in 1998 need only check out the size of the national debt in 1997 and 1998. The United States Treasury Department maintains a web site on the internet that provides public debt figures updated on a daily basis.

The total debt at the end of 1997 was $5,369.7 billion ($5.37 trillion). By the end of 1998, the debt had risen to $5,478.7 billion ($5.48 trillion). How could the national debt rise by $109 billion if the government had a $69.2 billion surplus? It couldn't. The United States Government had to borrow $30 billion to pay the on-budget deficit. In addition, since the Social Security Surplus was all invested in United States Treasury securities as required by law, the government's debt to the Social Security fund also went up.

How can anybody look at these figures and claim the government now has money to give away? How could anyone conclude that we now need to cut tax rates to an even lower level? Governor Bush has defended his plan to cut taxes by saying the "surplus belongs to the American people—not the government—and should be returned to the people." The only surplus that exists—the surplus in the Social Security Trust Fund—belongs neither to the government nor to the public at large. It belongs to the Trust Fund and to people who have faithfully made contributions to the Fund in the belief that the money would be somehow set aside to make sure that the Fund remained solvent.

Taking money that working Americans have contributed to the Social Security Trust Fund and using that money to finance a tax cut that would benefit mostly higher-income Americans, would result in an additional redistribution of income from lower-income Americans to higher-income Americans. At the same time, it would jeopardize both the solvency of the Social Security Trust Fund and the health of the American economy. The proposed tax cut is one of the most irresponsible proposals ever put forth by a presidential candidate in terms of its effect on government finances and the health of the economy.

The public debt, or the national debt as it is most often called, has increased by more than $4.6 trillion just during the past 19 years! It took over 200 years, from the nation's birth until 1981, to accumulate the first one trillion dollars of debt. However, by 1986 a second trillion dollars had been added to the debt, and by 1990 the debt exceeded the $3 trillion mark. In just nine years, 1981-1990, our government tripled the amount of the public debt!

These figures are not at all compatible with the public perception that the United States Government has a budget surplus and must decide whether to spend that surplus or give it back to the American people in the form of a tax cut. The harsh reality is that, despite all the publicity to the contrary, there is no real budget surplus in any meaningful sense of the term.

These numbers are definitely not consistent with the public rhetoric being delivered to the American people by both Al Gore and George W. Bush, not to mention the President of the United States. The two candidates disagree about what to do with the alleged surplus, but both are deliberately giving the impression that there is a large budget surplus. This is a cruel hoax being played on the American people by both presidential candidates as well as the President. In essence, Gore, Bush, and Clinton are deliberately misleading the American people on this issue. Although there are some exceptions, most of the news media are going along with the public pronouncements without questioning the accuracy of the candidates' statements. Most journalists do not have much formal training in economics and thus are hesitant to go out on a limb and question the validity of the public position of both candidates for the Presidency of the United States. The net result is a public perception that the government has excess money at a time when the federal indebtedness is more than five times as high as it was just 20 years ago!

The alleged budget surplus and its relationship to the Social Security Trust Fund will be covered in detail in the next two chapters. The remaining chapters of this book will be devoted to an overview of economic policies during the past 35 years with an emphasis on economic malpractice that I refer to as voodoo economics. The term, "voodoo economics," was coined by former President George Bush during his 1980 primary campaign battle against Ronald Reagan for the Republican presidential nomination. Candidate Bush referred to the economic package proposed by Reagan as "voodoo economics" which could lead to disaster if implemented.

After losing the nomination to Ronald Reagan, Bush retracted his negative characterization of Reagan's economic proposals and accepted the vice-presidential nomination. The new vice president then became a convert to the policies, which eventually came to be known as Reaganomics. In addition to supporting the policies during the Reagan years, Bush essentially practiced the same economic policies during his own term as President. This is reflected partly by the fact that the average on-budget deficit for his four years as president exceeded $286 billion per year, and the national debt grew by $1.4 trillion during his term.

For purposes of this book, I define voodoo economics as national economic policies which are based on unsound economic principles and which do not have the support of the majority of mainstream professional economists. If we use this definition, voodoo economics was practiced long before George Bush coined the phrase in 1980. Specifically, Lyndon B. Johnson practiced extremely unsound economic policies during the 1960s that inflicted great damage on the American economy. We will examine those policies in Chapter 6.

Before proceeding, I want to ask readers to consider the material in this book on its merits and not shy away from parts of it because it is not compatible with their political views or their personal assessments of the presidents involved. I do not have a partisan political agenda. I am a political independent who has never voted a straight party ticket. My parents were Republicans, and I voted for Richard Nixon in 1960 when he lost the race but did not vote for him either time he was elected.

I write this book as a professional economist with a Ph.D. degree in the field from Indiana University and a 25-year record of crusading for economic literacy in this country. I also write the book as a concerned citizen who sees the nation once again at a critical fork in the road where pursuing the wrong pathway could blow the golden opportunity that we once again have for long-term economic prosperity.

The nation faced similar forks in the road in 1965-66 and again in 1980. In my opinion, we chose to travel the wrong road in both of those instances primarily because the American people were misinformed. The consequences of both misdirected journeys were immeasurable. In 1965-66, it was a liberal Democrat who led us in the wrong direction. In 1980, it was a conservative Republican. Sound economic policies are neither Democratic nor Republican. It is possible to pursue equally sound economic policies while pursuing either a conservative or a liberal political agenda if the correct decisions are made in both cases.

But good economics and good politics are often in direct conflict, and when partisan politicians have to choose between the two they almost always choose good politics, even if it means misleading the American people and leading the nation in the wrong direction. Today, we have a third chance to choose between alternate economic roads. Either political party can lead us in the right direction, but in order to do so both parties must abandon some of the promises that they have already made and be honest with the American people for a change. Will we as a nation once again blow a golden opportunity for long-term prosperity because of our lack of knowledge of basic economic principles, and because politicians are taking advantage of our economic illiteracy and making unrealistic promises? Only time will tell.

EXHIBIT 1-1
NATIONAL DEBT BY FISCAL YEAR 1981-1999
IN BILLIONS OF DOLLARS

Year	Debt
1981	994.8
1982	1,137.3
1983	1,371.7
1984	1,564.7
1985	1,817.5
1986	2,120.6
1987	2,346.1
1988	2,601.3
1989	2,868.0
1990	3,206.6
1991	3,598.5
1992	4,002.1
1993	4,351.4
1994	4,643.7
1995	4,921.0
1996	5,181.9
1997	5,369.7
1998	5,478.7
1999	5.606.1

Source: Economic Report of the President, 2000

CHAPTER 2

THE ALLEGED BUDGET SURPLUS

In this chapter, we will examine the status of the federal government's operating budget over the past six decades. The "operating budget" which the government refers to as the "on-budget" includes all receipts and expenditures for government operations except those involving the Social Security Trust Fund.

Since the law requires that Social Security funds be kept separate from general government operating funds, the two funds are not to be commingled. As a result, the government releases budget-deficit or budget-surplus figures for the two funds separately. The on-budget deficit or surplus is the difference between government receipts and expenditures excluding the Social Security system.

For all practical purposes, the off-budget deficit or surplus is the deficit or surplus in the Social Security program. Technically, the United States Postal Service is also legally designated as "off-budget." However, since the Postal Service must maintain an approximately balanced budget in its operations, we can essentially equate the off-budget surplus or deficit with that of the Social Security system.

Thus, the on-budget deficit or surplus is a measure of whether the government is operating in the red or in the black, and the off-budget surplus or deficit is a measure of the solvency of the Social Security system. Unfortunately, despite the legal requirement that the two funds be kept separate, the government has devised a misleading measure called the "unified budget" which combines the two budget categories. By combining the two funds, a large surplus in the Social Security budget can more than offset the on-budget deficit and show a surplus in the unified budget. This is the primary trick that the government has been using to deceive the public into believing there is a surplus in the operating budget when there is not.

To verify this fact, readers can go to the internet website of the Office of Management and Budget, a division of the Executive Office of The President of the United States, and check out their publication, "A Citizen's Guide to the Federal Budget." Among the revelations of this official publication is the following statement.

> When the unified budget first booked a surplus of $69 billion in 1998, the on-budget accounts were still in deficit by $30 billion. In 1999, the unified budget ran a $124 billion surplus, nearly all of which was the result of the Social Security surplus. The on-budget accounts were almost exactly in balance.

Thus even the Executive Office of the President of the United States verifies that the only place there is a surplus is in the Social Security Trust Fund! Yet, on June 26, 2000, President Clinton announced a projected surplus of $1.9 trillion over the next decade. The announcement was made in such a way as to lead journalists to believe he was talking about a surplus in the operating budget. Below is a sample (from ABC News.com) of the way this story was reported to the public.

> WASHINGTON, June 26—Flush with cash from the soaring economy, the U.S. government has even more money to spend than was thought just a few months ago.
> President Clinton announced today that over the next decade, the federal budget surplus will total nearly $1.9 trillion.

That's more than 2 ½ time what the administration predicted it would be in February.

    "The American people should be very proud of this news," Clinton said as he announced the new numbers in the Rose Garden this afternoon. "It's the result of their hard work and their support for fiscal discipline. It's proof that we can create a better future for ourselves when we put our minds to it."

    ....But even as the president hailed the new numbers, he cautioned against making plans to spend all of the projected tax revenue.

    "This is just a budget projection," he said. "It would not be prudent to commit every penny of a future surplus that is just a projection and therefore subject to change."....

    "It would be a big mistake to commit this entire surplus to spending or tax cuts," Clinton said... "The projections could be wrong, they could be right."

President Clinton did the country a great disservice with that announcement. He knew how it would be interpreted by the media, and his motives for making the announcement were exclusively political. After 8 years of dealing with budget figures he had to know that the projections were definitely wrong. He also knew that whatever the size of any budget surpluses over the next decade, almost all of the money will belong to the Social Security program.

    Strangely enough, the announcement probably helped George W. Bush far more than it helped Gore. The same article from ABC News.com that was quoted above also gave the reaction of the Bush Camp.

    "Today's report confirms the accuracy of the conservative estimates Governor Bush used in preparing his balanced budget plan," said Bush spokesman Ari Fleischer. "The report also demonstrates the importance of passing the governor's tax cuts to prevent all this new money from being spent on bigger government."

    Such a statement is absolutely shocking. Does Governor Bush really believe that there is any new money except that resulting from the higher Social Security taxes which is earmarked for funding the retirement of the baby boomers? Is the governor totally unaware that the United States government has more than $4.5 trillion in unpaid bills just from the past twenty years of excess spending? Surely the younger Bush knows that his father's administration spent $1,145.1 billion more than it collected in revenue during President Bush's four-year term.

Why isn't George W. Bush trying to find ways to undo the damage done during the Reagan-Bush years by paying down at least part of the debt accumulated during those years of irresponsible deficit spending? Why would he call for additional tax cuts if he truly understood the government's financial condition?

Equally irresponsible are the statements of both President Clinton and Vice President Gore. It is easy to understand Gore's motivation. Like George W. Bush he is trying to ride the budget-surplus myth right into the White House. Gore feels he has to promise increased spending on domestic programs to get elected just as Governor Bush believes that his promised tax cuts will get him elected. Both are citing the mythical budget surplus as the source of funds to pay for their promises.

It is hard to understand why President Clinton is behaving so irresponsibly with regard to the budget-surplus myth. Despite the many personal shortcomings of his presidency, I do believe that historians will record that President Clinton did pursue sound economic policies throughout most of his presidency. He did manage to enact an unpopular tax increase "for the good of the economy" at the beginning of his term that partially replaced the lost revenue resulting from the Reagan tax cuts. At the time of the Clinton tax hike, it was widely predicted that his action would devastate the economy. Readers can judge for themselves whether or not that happened, but they cannot deny that the economy is currently in the longest expansion in history and the unemployment rate is at a 30-year low.

Neither can they deny that he inherited gigantic budget deficits and managed to pursue policies that resulted in an approximately balanced budget for 1999.

Given these facts, it is hard to understand why President Clinton is now behaving so irresponsibly in helping to feed the growing myth that the government has excess money. It seems that he should be urging caution and telling the American people that there is no surplus in the operating budget of the United States government. I believe that he is in a position to set the record straight, and I hope he will do so before election day, so that Gore and Bush can debate something other than how to use the nonexistent budget surplus. Perhaps Clinton is preoccupied with the public perception of his presidency and believes that by exaggerating his economic achievements he can enhance his public image during the last months of his presidency. If this is the case, historians will criticize him harshly for trying to take a final ego trip at the expense of the people and the future of the economy.

The one thing that is crystal clear to informed observers is that there is no budget surplus except that in the Social Security fund. This fact is confirmed by the Executive Office of the President as the excerpt from "A Citizen's Guide to the Federal Budget" (page 18) verifies. Given this fact, how can we possible justify using that Social Security money for either a tax cut or for new spending programs?

Using the surplus in the Social Security Trust Fund to finance a tax cut for the rich, or for increased government spending, would be like stealing from your mother's retirement fund to supplement your current income because Momma doesn't need that money right now. But since you are currently living beyond your means, Momma will question where you are going to get the money to repay her when she does need her money. Momma probably won't settle for the lame explanation that you will cross that bridge when you get to it. She's too smart for that. In fact, if you have borrowed from Momma's retirement fund in the past, she may now decide that because of your current fiscal irresponsibility she wants all her money back right now!

Of course, you might plead with Momma and tell her that a bunch of your friends who have done favors for you are expecting big gifts in return, and you can't find any way to pay for the gifts except by borrowing her retirement money. Or you might try shedding a few tears or throwing a temper tantrum in an effort to get Momma's sympathy for the fact that you don't earn enough money to live the life-style you'd really like to live so you want to borrow Momma's retirement money in order to live the higher life-style. But neither of these approaches is likely to cut much ice with Momma. After all, she wasn't born yesterday, and it is her hard-earned money that she has set aside for her old age.

An Overview of the
Federal Budget During the Past Six Decades

Table 2-1 reveals the budget history of the United States government from the 1940s to the 1990s, excluding the Social Security Trust Fund. As you can see, the nation experienced serious deficits and an escalation in the national debt during the 1940s because of the enormous cost of financing World War II. This was a case where there was no good alternative way of financing the War. Our very survival and the future of the nation were at stake. These circumstances mandated that we spend whatever was necessary to win the war. It was one of those times when the government had no choice but to borrow the needed money.

The average annual budget deficit for the 1940s was more than six times that of the 1950s and nearly three times the average deficit during the 1960s. This is what would be expected, and most people would probably agree that the deficit spending during World War II was justified.

However, all the deficit spending since that time, with the exception of necessary small deficits during recessions, represents fiscal irresponsibility.

The 1970s set a trend toward larger budget deficits and a substantial increase in the national debt. But deficit spending during the seventies was child's play compared to what took place in the 1980s and 1990s as our government seemed to lose all sense of fiscal responsibility and allowed deficit spending and growth in the national debt to go through the roof. The national debt skyrocketed by 575 percent between the end of the seventies and the end of the nineties. By contrast, the debt rose by only about 45 percent during the twenty-year period from the end of the 1940s to the end of the 1960s.

TABLE 2-1: FEDERAL GOVERNMENT
ON-BUDGET DEFICITS AND NATIONAL DEBT BY
DECADE 1940s—1990s IN BILLIONS OF DOLLARS

Decade	Total Deficits For Decade	Average Annual Deficit	National Debt at End of Decade
1940s	$187.7	$18.77	$252.6
1950s	29.3	2.93	287.5
1960s	65.2	6.52	365.8
1970s	353.8	35.38	829.5
1980s	1,688.7	168.87	2,868.0
1990s	2,032.5	203.25	5,606.1

Source: Economic Report of the President, 2000

Budget Deficits and Surpluses During the Seventies

Table 2-2 shows the on-budget deficits and the national debt from 1971 to 1980. As you can see, the deficit varied from year to year, going up in some years, and declining in other years. For example, the deficit declined from $26.4 billion in 1972 to $15.4 billion in 1973 and then further declined to $8.0 billion in 1974. However, as the economy plunged into recession, the deficit rose sharply because of increased automatic government spending for unemployment compensation and a reduction in tax revenue as unemployment rose and corporate profits fell. Most of the deficits during the 1970s can be attributed to the sluggish economy and the resulting rise in unemployment.

TABLE 2-2: FEDERAL GOVERNMENT
ON-BUDGET DEFICITS AND NATIONAL DEBT BY
FISCAL YEAR 1971-1980 IN BILLIONS OF DOLLARS

Year	On-budget Deficit	National Debt at End of Period
1971	26.1	408.2
1972	26.4	435.9
1973	15.4	466.3
1974	8.0	483.9
1975	55.3	541.9
1976	70.5	629.0
1977	49.8	706.4
1978	54.9	776.6
1979	38.7	829.5
1980	72.7	909.1

Source: Economic Report of the President, 2000

Budget Deficits and the National Debt
During the 1980s and 1990s

During the 1980 election campaign, candidate Ronald Reagan made one of the most irresistible promises ever made by any candidate for the presidency. He promised that if he were elected President, he would cut personal income tax rates by 30 percent over a three-year period.

"If I am elected President, I will cut personal income tax rates by 10 percent during my first year in office," Reagan promised the large crowd of enthusiastic supporters. As the applause began to build, Reagan raised his hand to quiet his admirers for a moment.

"Wait a minute," Mr. Reagan said. "I'm not done. I will cut your tax rates another 10 percent during my second year in office." This time Reagan allowed the cheers and applause to rise much higher before cutting them off.

"I have an encore," the candidate said as soon as the crowd was again quiet. "I will cut your tax rates an additional 10 percent during my third year for a total of 30 percent during my first three years as President!"

This time the crowd was allowed to cheer for as long as they wished. The "great communicator," with a lifetime of training and experience as a professional performer, was a master when it came to managing a crowd of enthusiastic supporters. And his message was sweeter than honey.

This performance was repeated again and again to crowds of enthusiastic supporters throughout the nation. And the good news didn't end with the promise of a 30 percent cut in tax rates. Candidate Reagan promised the crowds that he would simultaneously reduce both inflation and unemployment, avoid any major cuts in basic government services, build up the nation's military power, and "balance the federal budget by 1984."

Economists, including some recipients of the Nobel Prize, warned that Mr. Reagan could not deliver on these promises. And, during the Republican primary campaign, rival candidate George Bush referred to the economic package proposed by Reagan as "voodoo economics" which could lead to disaster if implemented. But millions of Americans found the Reagan promises so attractive that they elected him President in a massive landslide victory over incumbent President Jimmy Carter in the fall election.

On February 18, 1981, President Ronald Reagan delivered to a cheering joint session of Congress and a prime-time television audience a speech that marked a sharp turning point in American history. His "Program for

Economic Recovery" represented a radical departure from the political and economic thinking that had dominated the American government for the past 40 years.

Among other things, President Reagan called for passage of the controversial Kemp-Roth tax cut proposal that would cut personal income tax rates by 30 percent over a three-year period. As *Newsweek* magazine put it in its March 2, 1981 issue, "Reagan thus gambled the future—his own, his party's, and in some measure the nation's—on a perilous and largely untested new course called supply-side economics."

Many prominent economists warned that to follow the plan President Reagan had put forth would lead to huge budget deficits and could prove disastrous for the economy. But, despite such warnings, the Reagan Economic Program was put into effect. The President had been elected by an enormous margin and he felt he had a mandate from the people to do whatever he thought was best. Apparently the majority of Americans agreed, and the Congress—which was controlled by the Democrats at the time—enacted the Reagan proposals into law.

The results of the Reagan economic policies can be seen in Table 2-3. In just a little more than five years our government doubled the national debt. And instead of the promised balanced budget by 1984, the federal government ran a budget deficit of $185.7 billion in fiscal year 1984, and the deficit had reached $238 billion by fiscal year 1986. Although it had taken this nation more than 200 years to accumulate the first $1 trillion of national debt in late 1981, during the next 15 years the nation added an additional $4 trillion, bringing the total to $5 trillion by 1996!

TABLE 2-3: FEDERAL GOVERNMENT
ON-BUDGET DEFICITS AND NATIONAL DEBT BY
FISCAL YEAR 1981-1999 IN BILLIONS OF DOLLARS

Year	On-budget Deficit	National Debt at End of Period
1981	74.0	994.8
1982	120.1	1,137.3
1983	208.0	1,371.7
1984	185.7	1,564.7
1985	221.7	1,817.5
1986	238.0	2,120.6
1987	169.3	2,346.1
1988	194.0	2,601.3
1989	205.2	2,868.0
1990	277.8	3,206.6
1991	321.6	3,598.5
1992	340.5	4,002.1
1993	300.5	4,351.4
1994	258.9	4,643.7
1995	226.4	4,921.0
1996	174.1	5,181.9
1997	103.4	5,369.7
1998	30.0	5,478.7
1999	+ 0.7	5,606.1

Source: Economic Report of the President, 2000

How Economic Performance
Affects the Federal Budget

The performance of the economy is a major determinant of the size of the federal-budget deficit or surplus. The primary on-budget sources of revenue are the individual income tax and the corporation income tax. The revenue-generating capacity of both of these taxes is directly tied to the levels of spending in the economy and the unemployment rate. If the economy slips into a recession and consumer spending falls, corporate profits will drop sharply, and so will that portion of government revenue that is based on corporate profits.

Similarly, when sales decline, companies lay off workers, causing a rise in the unemployment rate. The unemployed workers stop paying individual income taxes which results in a decline in federal revenue from that source. In addition, the workers also begin drawing unemployment compensation which results in automatic increases in government spending.

Unemployed workers also sharply curtail their spending for goods and services because of their loss of income. When this happens, business sales decline even further, and employers lay off still more workers. It becomes a vicious cycle. A cutback in consumer spending causes businesses to lay off workers, resulting in a rise in the unemployment rate. A rise in the unemployment rate causes consumer spending to decline still further, leading to more layoffs.

When the unemployment rate is low and corporate profits are high, the federal government receives a healthy flow of revenue from both the individual income tax and the corporation income tax. However, when the economy is operating below the full-employment level with the unemployment rate rising, there is a decline in revenue and an increase in automatic spending for unemployment compensation, food stamps, and other similar programs. Thus, as the unemployment rate rises, so does the federal budget deficit.

Table 2-4 shows the relationship between the unemployment rate and the size of the federal budget deficit for the years 1981-1999. In 1990, the unemployment rate was 5.6 percent and the budget deficit $277.8 billion. The unemployment rate rose in both 1991 and 1992, and so did the deficit. The unemployment rate declined in every year after 1992, and so did the deficit.

TABLE 2-4: UNEMPLOYMENT RATES AND
FEDERAL GOVERNMENT ON-BUDGET DEFICITS
1981-1999

Year	Unemployment Rate (percent unemployed)	On-budget Deficit in Billions of Dollars
1981	7.6	74.0
1982	9.7	120.1
1983	9.6	208.0
1984	7.5	185.7
1985	7.2	221.7
1986	7.0	238.0
1987	6.2	169.3
1988	5.5	194.0
1989	5.3	205.2
1990	5.6	277.8
1991	6.8	321.6
1992	7.5	340.5
1993	6.9	300.5
1994	6.1	258.9
1995	5.6	226.4
1996	5.4	174.1
1997	4.9	103.4
1998	4.5	30.0
1999	4.2	+0.7

SOURCE: Economic Report of the President, 2000

It is extremely important to note that the government was unable to eliminate the deficit in any year prior to 1999 when the unemployment rate was at a 30-year low. Even in 1997 when the unemployment rate dropped below the 5 percent rate for the first time in 24 years, our government still had an on-budget deficit of $103.4 billion. The tax structure could not generate enough revenue to approximately balance the budget until 1999 when the unemployment rate had dipped all the way down to 4.2 percent.

The economy will not continue to operate at its current peak level of performance indefinitely. The economy always peaks out at the end of an expansion and enters the next phase of the business cycle, which is the contraction or recession. It is possible that by the time this book is published, the economy will have slipped into a mild recession. If not, it is only a matter of time until we will experience a recession.

Throughout American history, the economy has alternated between recession and prosperity following a pattern that economists call business cycles. There are generally four phases to the business cycle: (1) the expansion, (2) the peak, (3) the contraction, and (4) the trough. The last contraction (recession) in the United States lasted from July 1990 to May 1991 at which time the contraction bottomed out and a new expansion began. At the time of this writing, June 2000, the expansion is in its 111th consecutive month. Thus, this expansion is now longer than the previous all-time record expansion of 106 consecutive months from February 1961 to December 1969, and it is very likely to run its course at some point in the not too distant future.

Just as we can never predict exactly when a long dry period will end and the rains will come again, we can never predict with a high degree of accuracy when a business expansion will end and a new recession will begin. However, we can be absolutely sure that the expansion will end and the unemployment rate will once again rise. This has happened throughout history and will continue to happen into the foreseeable future. A recession that follows a long expansion does not have to be a severe recession. If the proper economic policies are followed, the recession can be short and mild, but rarely has that happened in the past.

As the long expansion of the 1960s continued month after month and year after year, some people speculated that perhaps the business cycle was a thing of the past, but they were wrong. That expansion was ended by a recession that lasted from December 1969 until November 1970, and there have been four additional recessions since then, including the severe recessions of 1973-74 and 1981-82. The 1973-74 recession was at the time the worst economic downturn since the Great Depression of the 1930s. The unemployment rate reached a high of 9 percent during that recession, the highest since the Great Depression. But the recession that took place during the early part of the Reagan administration dwarfed the recession of 1973-74. In the 1981-82 recession, the unemployment rate peaked out at 10.8 percent, and the average unemployment rates for the years 1982 and 1983 were 9.7 percent and 9.6 percent respectively.

Those who are projecting large budget surpluses in the years ahead based on the assumption that the current expansion will go on and on would do well to examine the above numbers. Just as the long expansion of the 1960s did not signal an end to business cycles, the current record expansion will also come to an end. Whether we will experience only mild recessions in the future instead of severe recessions like those of the 1970s and 1980s will depend largely on the quality of government economic policies. If politicians who have no understanding of basic economics again call the shots on economic policy, we could have results similar to those that followed the long expansion of the 1960s. On the other hand, with sound economic policies, we can minimize the severity of future recessions.

One basic change that may make future business cycles less severe and erratic than those of the past is the world economy that we now live in. Businesses no longer have to rely totally on American consumers to keep their sales up. As the volume of international trade has grown and markets have extended beyond national boundaries, the economy has become less prone to severe recessions.

How Federal Budget Policies Affect
The Performance of the Economy

The economy is highly sensitive to what economists call aggregate demand. Aggregate demand is the level of total spending in the economy which includes consumer spending, business spending for investment, government spending, and net exports. Essentially, in the long run the economy produces just as many goods and services as can be sold. An individual business firm will curtail production when sales decline, and the firm will expand production when sales rise. The level of production for a firm is determined by the level of sales.

Similarly, the economy as a whole curtails production when aggregate demand declines and expands production when aggregate demand rises. The federal government plays a major role in determining the level of aggregate demand and thus the performance of the economy. Therefore, decisions involving government spending and taxing policies must take into consideration the effect that these decisions will have on the performance of the economy.

An increase in government spending means an increase in aggregate demand, and a decrease in government spending means a decrease in aggregate demand unless there is an offsetting change in consumer and/or investment spending. When taxes are raised or lowered the level of after-tax income of consumers is changed, thus affecting the consumer-spending component of aggregate demand. When individual income tax rates are increased, consumers have less after-tax income to spend which will cause a decrease in consumer spending. When tax rates are lowered, consumers have more after-tax income to spend, and consumer spending is likely to rise.

Whether a change in consumer spending is good or bad for the economy depends on the current performance of the economy. If the economy is in recession with high unemployment, a rise in spending is just what is needed. However, if the economy is booming at the top of an expansion where any increase in aggregate demand may trigger inflation, which in turn can cause the economy to plunge into recession, increases in consumer spending have a detrimental effect.

At the time of this writing the economy is so overheated that the Federal Reserve System has been raising interest rates over and over in an attempt to cool it down and prevent a surge in inflation which could abort the expansion. Thus, one of the worst things the government could do at this time would be to cut taxes, giving consumers more after-tax income with which to increase spending. Yet, presidential candidate George W. Bush is proposing a large tax cut. The timing just couldn't be worse. In addition to throwing the economy off course, the cut in taxes would result in higher budget deficits and still larger increases to the national debt.

The proposal seems to be based exclusively on political considerations with no thought given to its impact on the economy. Just as a doctor must be concerned about possible side effects when he or she prescribes a potent medication for a patient, policy makers must always consider the economic impact of their political proposals.

Tax cuts are always popular, and tax hikes are always unpopular. The massive tax cuts during the Reagan administration plunged us into an ocean of red ink and caused the national debt to skyrocket. The tax increases at the beginning of the Clinton administration partly repaired the damage to the nation's tax structure and led to declining budget deficits including an approximately balanced operating budget for fiscal year 1999.

But we must not lose focus on the fact that the balanced budget was attainable only when the unemployment rate was at a 30-year low. The unemployment rate will rise again as it has always done during the contraction phase of the business cycle which always follows the end of an economic expansion. And when unemployment rises, so will the size of the budget deficits even if there are no further tax cuts. If we do have additional tax cuts, the deficits will be even higher.

In summary, there is no on-budget surplus with the exception of a reported tiny $0.7 billion for fiscal 1999, and there is unlikely to be any sizeable surpluses in the future. The nation has accumulated massive increases in the national debt during the past 20 years as a result of huge budget deficits year after year. Those who talk about a budget surplus are talking about the planned temporary surplus in the Social Security Trust Fund. We will address that issue in the following chapter.

CHAPTER 3

THE SOCIAL SECURITY TRUST FUND

The United States was one of the last advanced nation's in the world to establish a social security system. In a speech to Congress on January 17, 1935, President Franklin D. Roosevelt urged passage of the Social Security Act. Roosevelt said, "It is a sound idea—a sound ideal. Most of the other advanced countries of the world have already adopted it and their experience affords the knowledge that social insurance can be made a sound and workable project."

President Roosevelt stressed the importance of developing a "self-sustaining" system whose funds would be separate from general government financing. He said, "The system adopted, except for the money necessary to initiate it, should be self-sustaining in the sense that funds for the payment of insurance benefits should not come from the proceeds of general taxation."

With passage of the Social Security Act of 1935, America joined the rest of the advanced world in making a commitment to provide a financially sound social security system that would at least take some of the worry out of the financial consequences of growing old. Until recent decades, Americans have felt confident that their retirement benefits would be available when they needed them. They trusted their government to manage the funds wisely and responsibly. However, the events of the past 20 years have led many Americans to question the commitment of current politicians to keeping the fund solvent for future generations. The Social Security program has to some degree become a source of political maneuvering and a mask for irresponsible fiscal policies. Most of the abuse and misuse of the Social Security Trust Fund followed passage of legislation in 1983 which was supposed to raise—not lower—confidence in the long-term solvency of the program.

The Social Security Amendments of 1983

In 1983, legislation was enacted to improve the solvency of the Social Security Trust Fund which had run small budget deficits for seven years in a row from 1976-1982. The legislation, was in response to a recommendation the previous year by a Presidential Commission headed by Alan Greenspan. It was designed specifically for the purpose of building up a surplus in the Trust Fund in preparation for the staggering new obligations the fund would face when the baby-boom generation begins retiring about 2010. Both Social Security tax rates and the Social Security tax base were gradually raised over a seven-year period so the Trust Fund would be solvent when it took the big financial hit resulting from the retirement of the baby boomers, the largest generation in American history.

Unfortunately, instead of using the increased Social Security revenue to build up the size of the Trust Fund for future retirees as was intended, the government began using the surplus to fund other government programs as soon as it first appeared in 1983, and it has continued to do so ever since. This practice has masked the true size of federal budget deficits because each year since 1983 the government subtracted the surplus in the Social Security Trust Fund from the deficit in the operating budget and reported an official budget deficit that was billions of dollars below the actual deficit.

This issue came to a head in 1990 when Senator Daniel Patrick Moynihan of New York sent shock waves throughout Washington and much of the nation with his proposal to cut Social Security taxes. Senator Moynihan had been a strong supporter of the 1983 efforts to strengthen the Social Security system. He had served on the commission that recommended the plan that involved gradually raising the Social Security tax rate from 6.7 percent in 1983 to 7.65 percent in 1990, and raising the tax base from $35,700 in 1983 to $51,300 in 1990.

Senator Moynihan was outraged that, instead of being used to build up the size of the Social Security Trust Fund for future retirees as was intended, the surplus in the Social Security Fund was being used to pay for general government spending by investing it in Treasury Securities. Senator Moynihan, who felt the American people were being betrayed and deceived, proposed undoing the 1983 legislation by cutting Social Security taxes and returning the system to a "pay-as-you-go" basis which would have provided only enough revenue to take care of current retirees.

Moynihan took the position that if the government couldn't keep its hands out of the Social Security cookie jar, the jar should be emptied so there would be no Social Security surplus. He thought it was very dangerous and deceptive for the government to use the surplus in the Social Security Trust Fund to pay for general government spending, and thus proposed cutting Social Security taxes so there would be no surplus to mask the enormous deficits in the operating budget.

Cutting Social Security taxes wasn't really what Moynihan wanted. He had been a member of the Presidential Commission that had recommended the higher taxes, and he was a strong supporter of the legislation that enacted the higher taxes for purposes of strengthening the solvency of the Social Security Trust Fund. What Moynihan was really doing was blowing the whistle on the government for using the surplus for general government spending and then giving the impression that the deficit in the government's operating budget was tens of billions of dollars below what it actually was.

President Bush, who had said over and over on the campaign trail, "Read my lips. No new taxes," opposed Senator Moynihan's plan to cut Social Security taxes. If the government had not had the Social Security surplus from which to borrow, it would have been forced to either raise taxes or report much larger budget deficits to the public. In response to reporters' questions about Senator Moynihan's proposal to cut Social Security taxes, Bush replied, "It is an effort to get me to raise taxes on the American people by the charade of cutting them, or cut benefits, and I am not going to do it to the older people of this country."

But President Bush was in fact taking money from a fund that was supposed to be used to provide for "the older people of this country" and using it to fund general government. During George Bush's four years as President, the Social Security Trust Fund ran surpluses totaling $211.7 billion. Every dollar of that Social Security surplus was borrowed and used by the Bush administration to fund other government programs. Since not a penny of that debt was repaid during the Bush Presidency, higher taxes will have to be levied against the American people at some point in the future partly to repay the money that the "Read-my-lips-no-new-taxes" president borrowed from the Social Security Fund.

President Bush continued a practice that had begun during the second Reagan term and has continued through the Clinton-Gore years. That practice is to spend the dollars generated by Social Security taxes just like any other taxes even though Social Security funds are required by law to be kept separate from other funds. Earlier presidents did not have an opportunity to deceive the American people in this way. Even during the first four years of the Reagan administration, the Social Security system ran a net deficit of $12.4 billion. However, during Reagan's second term the Social Security system had a total surplus of $84.5 billion.

The Social Security surpluses continued to grow throughout the Clinton-Gore years. In 1999, the surplus in the Social Security budget reached a record high of $123.7 billion, most of which was used to fund general government operations. The general operating budget was balanced in 1999, with an official tiny on-budget surplus of $0.7 billion, for the first time in 39 years. Like Al Gore and George W. Bush, President Clinton had plenty of suggestions as to how to spend the Social Security surplus money.

One of the reasons that it has been so easy for the past three presidents to deceive the American people about the true financial condition of the United States Government is the fact that any Social Security surplus funds are by law supposed to be invested in U.S. Treasury securities. Under current law, the Social Security funds cannot be invested in stocks, bonds or even FDIC insured bank accounts. They must be invested in Treasury securities.

However, this does not in any way necessitate or justify the using of surplus funds to finance general government operations. Every dollar of Social Security revenue in excess of what is required to pay current benefits should be used to pay down the gigantic national debt. Doing so would have the equivalent effect of putting the money into a separate bank account that was off limits to politicians who were tempted to borrow the funds to pay for general government operations. Using Social Security funds to pay down the national debt during the Social Security surplus years between now and 2015, and then borrowing those dollars back during the deficit years that will come after 2015, would be the fiscally responsible thing to do. The surplus monies would be invested in government securities as required by law, but they would not be available for funding general government programs.

No president prior to Ronald Reagan had access to surplus Social Security revenue so there was not a temptation to violate the spirit of the law that requires Social Security funds to be kept separate from general government revenue. However, during the second term of the Reagan administration, $84.5 billion in Social Security surplus funds became available, and these funds were used, in violation of the spirit of the law, to fund general government operations and mask the true size of the federal deficit.

Reagan's successor, George Bush, had even more Social Security surplus money available to divert into the coffers of general government revenue, and President Bush diverted the entire $211.7 billion. Although President Clinton did reduce the huge budget deficits by raising income taxes and promoting a prosperous economy that resulted in eliminating the on-budget deficit in 1999, he also participated in the charade that portrayed government finances as being much better than they actually were. And Clinton also used the Social Security surpluses for general government financing.

America cannot afford to allow this charade to continue anymore. The time for truth is at hand. Al Gore and George W. Bush must be honest with the American people and acknowledge the true condition of the Government's finances. The people must be told that just during the past 20 years the government has accumulated more than $4.6 trillion in unpaid bills. Therefore, if there are any annual surpluses in the operating budget of the United States government in future years that money should be used to pay down the enormous debt. The public is entitled to know that 1999 was the first year in 39 years in which the government did not have an on-budget deficit, and that was due primarily to the fact that the unemployment rate was at a 30-year low.

Gore has pledged part of the surplus funds to paying down the debt, but he has also promised substantial increased spending for government programs. There is no money for such spending unless Gore wishes to raise taxes. He should get his hands completely out of the Social Security cookie jar and tell the people the truth about the alleged surplus.

It would be politically difficult for George W. Bush to withdraw his promise to cut taxes because it is almost the centerpiece of his campaign. But if he does not withdraw it prior to the election, and if he is elected, he should certainly tell the people the truth after the election. To implement a major tax cut at this time would inflict great damage on the economy and on government finances.

The American people must challenge the two candidates to stop deceiving the public with regard to the alleged budget surplus and lay out the hard facts about the massive growth in the national debt during the past 20 years. Surely both candidates know that they are misleading the American people. It would be down right scary to discover that one or both of the candidates for the Presidency of the United States knew so little about economics and the federal budget that they actually believed what they are telling the voters. It is almost equally disturbing to accept the notion that they do know the truth and are deliberately misleading the public.

Table 3-1 shows how the surplus in the Social Security Trust Fund served to mask the true size of the deficit in the government's operating budget. As you can see, the Social Security (off-budget) surplus was nonexistent until 1983 and, for all practical purposes, was insignificant until 1985 when it reached the $9.4 billion level as the increased Social Security tax dollars flowed into the Trust Fund. Five years later, in 1990, the surplus had soared to $56.6 billion. That is when the political fireworks began. There was a $277.8 billion deficit in the government's operating budget that year, and every penny of the Social Security surplus was used to help finance the huge on-budget deficit.

TABLE 3-1: ON-BUDGET AND OFF-BUDGET
SURPLUSES OR DEFICITS, 1976-1999, IN BILLIONS
OF DOLLARS

Year	On-budget Surplus(+) or Deficit(-)	Off-budget Surplus(+) or Deficit(-)
1976	-70.5	-3.2
1977	-49.8	-3.9
1978	-54.9	-4.3
1979	-38.7	-2.0
1980	-72.7	-1.1
1981	-74.0	-5.0
1982	-120.1	-7.9
1983	-208.0	+0.2
1984	-185.7	+0.3
1985	-221.7	+9.4
1986	-238.0	+16.7
1987	-169.3	+19.6
1988	-194.0	+38.8
1989	-205.2	+52.8
1990	-277.8	+56.6
1991	-321.6	+52.2
1992	-340.5	+50.1
1993	-300.5	+45.3
1994	-258.9	+55.7
1995	-226.4	+62.4
1996	-174.1	+66.6
1997	-103.4	+81.4
1998	-30.0	+99.2
1999	+0.7	+123.7

Source: Economic Report of the President, 2000

Changes in Social Security's Treatment
Under the Budget Enforcement Act of 1990

The Budget Enforcement Act of 1990 made substantial changes in the budget process. Among these changes was the removal of the income and outgo of the social security trust funds from all calculations of the Federal budget, including the budget deficit or surplus. This exclusion applied to the budget prepared by the President, the Federal budgets formulated by the Congress, and to the budget process provisions designed to reduce and control the budget deficits.

The Social Security Trust Fund was always supposed to be kept separate from the government's operating budget. However, in 1969, a time when Congress did not have a budget-making process, President Lyndon Johnson administratively began officially counting Social Security funds as part of the Federal Budget. In 1974, with passage of the Congressional Budget and Impoundment Control Act, Congress adopted a process for developing budget goals and these also officially counted Social Security as part of the "unified budget."

These actions did not set well with the public, and Senator Moynihan's efforts to make the public aware of just how the Social Security money was being used led to concerns that the public's confidence in the program was being eroded. The increased public awareness also led to proposals to legally remove social security from the budget. Finally, in 1990, Congress reacted to the criticism that surplus social security taxes were masking the size of the budget deficits by legally removing Social Security from the budget calculations.

Despite these actions, both candidates for the Presidency of the United States are making all sorts of promises based on the impression that there is a surplus in the operating budget of the United States government. There is no such surplus. The only surplus is in the Social Security Trust Fund which is legally supposed to be off limits. American voters must keep in mind that it is the Social Security nest egg that the candidates are talking about, even if the candidates aren't willing to admit it.

Where Do Surplus Social Security Tax Receipts Go?

In fiscal year 1998, the federal government collected $99.2 billion more in Social Security taxes than it paid out in Social Security benefits. What happened to the huge surplus? The same thing that happens to all surplus Social Security taxes—the money was used to pay for other government programs.

According to a Congressional Research Bulletin, *Social Security: Surplus Receipts Trigger New Financing Debate,* dated May 6, 1991, "Once the taxes are received, they become indistinguishable from other monies paid into the Treasury and are used to pay other Government obligations." Most people probably envision their Social Security contributions being put into a separate fund which could not be touched by politicians or Treasury Department officials. But it doesn't work that way.

Social security taxes, like all other Government revenues, are deposited in the U.S. Treasury. Each day, Social Security contributions flow into approximately 15,000 depository accounts maintained by the Government with financial institutions throughout the nation and, along with other forms of tax revenue, become part of the Government's operating cash pool. The Treasury makes separate accounting entries for social security taxes. In other words, the government keeps a record of how much money is supposed to be in the Trust Fund. Similarly, Social Security benefits are paid from the Treasury, not from the trust funds. Essentially, the only way that Social Security receipts and payments are kept separate from other government financing, is through bookkeeping entries by the U.S. Treasury.

There is a little more to it than this, but not much more. Government IOUs called "special issues of the Treasury" are posted to the account of the Social Security Trust Fund. These "special-issue" securities have no commercial value because they cannot be sold in the marketplace. When social security benefits are paid out, a corresponding amount of securities are deducted from the Trust Fund.

The Congressional Research Bulletin referred to above states, "That more social security taxes were received than spent is merely reflected in a higher balance of securities on the trust fund ledgers. In essence, the trust funds represent a form of IOU—a promise by the Government that, in order to pay social security benefits, it will obtain resources in the future equal to the value of the securities."

By law, Social Security Trust Fund surpluses are supposed to be invested in U.S. Treasury securities. Such securities are supposed to be the safest of all investments, and interest is paid to holders of Treasury securities. The only catch is that the Government pays interest on funds borrowed from the Social Security Trust Fund by posting "special-issue" securities just like the ones posted when the money was borrowed. This means that both the assets and the earnings of the Social Security Trust Fund are in the form of Government IOUs that have no commercial value.

Where Will the Government Get the Money to Repay the Social Security Trust Fund?

It is estimated that by the year 2015 the glut of baby boom retirees will have wiped out the surplus in the Social Security Trust Fund, and that it will begin running deficits on a regular basis. This means that the social security program will need the surplus funds that were built up in past years and loaned to the Government for other spending programs.

Thus, not only will there no longer be a Social Security surplus for the Government to borrow, but the Government will have to find some way of raising the funds to pay back the Social Security money that it has borrowed. Given the fact that the U.S. Government has been unable to balance its budget for the past 30 years, even in those years when it was able to borrow social security surplus funds, how in the world will the government manage to balance the budget in the future and also pay back past borrowed funds? That is a question that all Americans should ask both themselves and those politicians who are behaving as if the nation had more money than it knows what to do with.

The hard facts are that it will be extremely difficult for the government to raise funds to pay down its debt to the Social Security Fund. It will either have to raise taxes substantially or borrow the money from the public who will not settle for Government IOUs with no commercial value. Given these hard alternatives, there will almost certainly be some political leaders who will suggest cutting Social Security benefits instead of raising taxes.

What Happens if the Government Cannot Repay its Debt to the Social Security System?

If the government does not fully repay its obligations to the Social Security Trust Fund with interest whenever they are needed, benefits would have to be reduced. The Social Security Fund is not actuarially sound on a long-term basis even if the government repays all it owes with interest. The following direct quote from the Social Security Administration's *2000 OASDI Trustees Report* reveals just how crucial the government's ability and willingness to repay its debt to the Social Security Trust Fund is to the solvency of the Fund.

"Under the intermediate assumptions, OASDI tax revenues are estimated to exceed expenditures until 2015. ... Total income (including interest earnings on the trust funds) will exceed expenditures through 2024. It is estimated that beginning in 2025, trust fund assets would have to be redeemed to cover the difference until the assets of the combined funds are exhausted in 2037."

With the retirement of baby boomers starting in about 2010, Social Security benefit payments will begin to soar, and five years later the Social Security fund will begin running growing annual deficits. The interest earnings from past surpluses will keep the fund afloat for awhile, but it is estimated that beginning in 2025, it will be necessary for the government to start repaying the money it owes the Social Security Trust Fund in order for the fund to remain solvent.

Finally in 2037, even if the government has repaid every penny it owes the Social Security system along with interest by that date, the Fund will no longer be able to pay full benefits. At that time, it is estimated that the Social Security System would be receiving only enough revenue to cover 72 percent of its annual obligations and would have no reserve to fall back on.

What these facts tell us is that the government must repay every dollar it has borrowed from the Social Security Trust Fund, with interest, over the next 37 years. And even then, without major Social Security reform, the fund will become insolvent.

At the end of 1999, the government owed the Social Security System approximately $2,088 billion (or $2.09 trillion) and was continuing to borrow from the fund at an alarming rate. The government has been borrowing and spending every penny of the Social Security surplus. Where is the government going to get the money to operate when it can no longer borrow from Social Security? More importantly, how is the government going to pay back all that it already owes the Social Security fund?

Government Options

Since the government is going to have to gradually come up with enormous additional resources over the next 37 years, what are its options? It can borrow larger and larger sums from the public. It can borrow enough initially to replace the funds that it has been borrowing annually from Social Security, and then later borrow even larger sums from the public to gradually pay back the money it owes Social Security. This seems to be what short-sighted politicians are counting on.

However, given the fact that the government has added nearly 5 times as much to the national debt during the past 20 years as was accumulated during the previous 200 years of American history, this does not seem to be a viable option. The nation just keeps getting deeper and deeper into debt, borrowing both for operating expenses and to pay the massive interest payments on the debt. This cannot go on indefinitely without severe consequences.

Perhaps it is time to cut off the government's easy access to credit. And maybe we should insist that the government keep its spending within the bounds of its income over the long run like individuals and businesses must do. If the government were to be so disciplined as to rule out borrowing Social Security surplus funds, then the funding for any new programs would have to come from decreased spending and/or higher taxes.

Is either of the candidates for president proposing decreased spending and/or higher taxes? No. They are proposing just the opposite! George W. Bush wants to reduce government revenue even farther by cutting taxes, and Al Gore has plans to increase government spending. Both candidates are planning to use the temporary surplus in Social Security as the source for funding their plans, but they are not being honest with the voters.

Bush is promising tax cuts and Gore is promising new spending programs, but neither is telling the people that the financing of these programs will come from borrowed Social Security funds. Nor are they informing voters that when the borrowed Social Security funds are repaid, taxes will almost certainly have to be raised.

There seems to be something a little sinister about current politicians keeping taxes down in the present by borrowing tomorrow's money. Such action will result in future politicians having to raise taxes to pay for the excesses of their predecessors.

CHAPTER 4

HOW THE ECONOMY WORKS

This chapter and the following chapter are designed to give the reader some familiarity with how the American economy is supposed to operate so you can better understand the severe consequences of economic malpractice. Without a basic understanding of how the economy operates, we cannot make sound judgments as to which economic proposals put forth by the politicians are in fact based on sound economic principles and which ones represent voodoo economics. It is absolutely crucial to the future of our economy that government officials, civic leaders, journalists, and others who help mold public opinion become familiar with the basic principles in these two chapters.

First of all, policy makers must have accurate measures of the economy's performance in order to formulate sound economic policies. There are several such measures, but probably the most important is the gross domestic product usually referred to as the GDP. This is a measure of the total production of goods and services in the economy in a year's time.

The Concept of GDP

Specifically, the gross domestic product is defined as *the total dollar value of all goods and services produced in a year's time, within a country's borders, measured in terms of their market prices.* The GDP tells policy makers how well the economy is doing. In a sense, GDP numbers are like the speedometer on a car. They tell us whether the economy is growing too fast, too slowly, or at the appropriate rate for sustained prosperity.

The government uses the dollar value of all goods and services produced in calculating the GDP, instead of just adding up the physical numbers of all the items produced, because a tally of the total production in physical numbers would be useless in making comparisons. In order to better understand the need to convert all production into dollar terms, let's look at an example of a single production unit that produces more than one product.

Suppose that a farmer produces three different crops (corn, soybeans, and wheat) on his farm. Now let's suppose that last year he produced 20,000 bushels of corn, 8,000 bushels of soybeans, and 10,000 bushels of wheat. This year, he varied the acreage devoted to each crop, and yields per acre were slightly different from last year. The net result was that this year he produced 18,000 bushels of corn, 10,000 bushels of soybeans, and 11,000 bushels of wheat. Did the farmer have a better year this year or last year? We can't tell with only this much information. Although the farmer produced less corn this year than last, he had an increase in the production of both soybeans and wheat this year. Since the market price per bushel for each of these grains is different, the only way we can tell which year was better for the farmer is to calculate the total dollar value of grain produced in each of the two years.

What is true for this individual farmer is true for the economy as a whole. We must convert the production of each and every good and service produced in the economy into a common measure (dollar value) in order to determine whether the economy as a whole did better last year or this year. Since we use the market price (the actual price that items sell for) to determine their dollar value, we avoid the problem of having to estimate the value of items except for a few rare exceptions.

Determining the Level of GDP

The size and the rate of growth of the GDP are very important because they are the major determinants of the standard of living. If the GDP grows too slowly, or actually declines, there will be an increase in the number of people unemployed, whereas, if it grows too rapidly, increased inflation may occur. What determines the level of GDP? The answer to this question is that the level of total spending in the economy is the primary determinant of the level of GDP.

As a first step in understanding how the level of total spending in the economy determines the level of GDP, let's see how the level of total production is determined in a single factory. Suppose you own and operate a small manufacturing plant that produces quality bookcases. You have a number of distributors for your product and, for quite some time, you have been producing and selling approximately 500 bookcases per week. Since you know that the demand for your product can fluctuate up or down, you maintain an inventory of 400 bookcases in a warehouse. Thus, if there should be a sudden increase in the demand for your product to 600 bookcases per week, you could sell from your reserve inventory, as well as from current production, temporarily. However, the warehouse reserves will last for only four weeks should the demand continue at 600 bookcases per week. Therefore, you will probably hire additional workers and increase current production to 600 bookcases per week if the demand remains at that level for very long.

Now suppose that just the opposite occurs. After being able to sell 500 bookcases per week for more than a year, sales suddenly begin to decline and demand soon falls to only 400 bookcases per week. You will not continue to produce 500 bookcases per week, indefinitely, if you are able to sell only 400 per week. As unpleasant as it may be, you will need to consider laying off some of your workers and reducing production to 400 bookcases per week so that production will again be in balance with sales. In summary, the number of bookcases you will produce per week will be determined by the number you can sell. If customers increase their purchases of bookcases, you will increase production. But, if they reduce purchases, you will reduce production accordingly. Over the long run, you will produce just about as many bookcases as you can sell.

What is true for an individual factory is true for the economy as a whole. Just as you will increase or decrease production, and the size of your work force, depending on the level of sales, the economy as a whole will adjust production, and the number of workers employed, when the level of total spending rises or falls. In other words, if total spending in the economy increases, total production (GDP), and the number of workers employed, will also rise. On the other hand, if total spending decreases, total production (GDP) and employment will decline.

The total spending in the economy is made up of the combined spending of three different sectors of the economy. They are consumer spending, investment spending, and government spending. There is also a foreign sector. However, in order to keep our analysis as simple as possible, we will assume that imports of goods and services from foreign countries are offset by an equal amount of exports of goods and services to foreign countries. In this case, consumer spending, plus investment spending, plus government spending would make up 100 percent of net total spending in the economy. As you probably know, imports and exports are not in balance today. However, over the long run, they have roughly canceled one another out, and hopefully this will become true again in the future.

In any case, by making the assumption that exports equal imports, we are able to provide a much clearer analysis of how the economy operates.

Because the three major components of total spending are so important, we want to examine each one in some detail. We will look at the factors that determine the amount of spending in each category as well as the effects of each component on GDP.

Consumer Spending

Consumer spending, usually referred to simply as *consumption* by economists, involves the purchase of consumer goods and services. These are things that consumers buy for their own personal use such as food, clothing, appliances, haircuts, entertainment, and medical care. Consumer spending is the largest of the three components of total spending, accounting for more than 60 percent of GDP. Since consumption is such a large portion of the total spending, changes in consumption have a much greater effect on the level of GDP than changes in the other two components. Let's examine some of the determinants of the amount of consumer spending that will take place.

Income. The most important determinant of consumer spending is income. Increases in income almost always lead to increased consumption, while decreases in income usually result in reduced consumption. If the GDP is rising, and more and more unemployed workers are finding jobs, there will be an increase in income that in turn will lead to an increase in consumer spending. This increase in consumer spending will lead to an even larger GDP and thus more jobs and income. This cycle can continue until the economy reaches the full-employment level of GDP which is the point where all productive resources are being utilized. Any increase in spending beyond this level will lead to increased inflation.

Let's look at the opposite situation. Suppose that, at a time when the economy is operating at the full-employment level, the GDP begins to decline. This decline in GDP will cause workers to lose their jobs and will thus reduce income. The reduction in income will cause a decrease in consumer spending which will cause GDP to decline even more, and will result in still more workers losing their jobs and thus suffering reductions in income. The longer this downward cycle is allowed to continue, the greater the unemployment rate.

Economists use the term, **recession**, to describe periods when the GDP is declining and unemployment is rising. Usually, if the GDP declines continuously for a period of six months, the economy is considered to be in a recession. If the GDP falls and remains at a very low level for a prolonged period, while large numbers of people are unemployed, the economy is in a **depression.**

Expectations. Consumers' expectations about the future of the economy play a major role in determining the amount of money they will spend. If individuals believe the economy will soon go into a recession and they will lose their jobs, they may cut back substantially on their spending. This can be a very dangerous thing. If enough people simultaneously become convinced that a recession is on the way, and if they behave accordingly, they can bring on the very recession that they fear. Why is this true? Because, if people believe there will soon be a recession that will cause them to lose their jobs, they will cut back on spending and begin saving their money for use when the recession occurs. In other words, they will not buy the new automobiles, refrigerators, television sets, and so forth that they were planning to buy. As orders coming into factories for such items decline, employers will reduce production and lay off workers. These unemployed workers will then reduce their spending because of a lack of income and, as a result, still more workers will lose their jobs.

Consumer spending can also be affected by expectations of future inflation. The fear of increased inflation can cause consumers to behave in such a way that they actually contribute to the inflation they fear. If they believe there will be substantial price increases in the near future, they may go on a spending spree in an effort to buy as many consumer goods and services as possible before these items become so expensive they can no longer afford them. However, the increased demand for goods and services will cause prices to rise even higher.

Taxes. Taxes affect consumer spending because they determine the amount of after-tax income people have to spend. An increase in taxes will result in a reduction in after-tax income and thus a reduction in consumer spending. Similarly, a decrease in taxes will give consumers an increase in after-tax income, and will thus result in increased spending. This relationship between taxes and consumer spending provides the government with a potential device for regulating the level of the GDP. By reducing taxes and giving the people more money to spend, the government could raise the level of the GDP. On the other hand, if the government wanted to reduce the rate of growth of the GDP, it could raise taxes and thus reduce the spending power of consumers.

Investment Spending

Investment spending, usually referred to simply as *investment* by economists, refers to business spending for such things as new factories, machines, store buildings, and so forth, which will ultimately increase the productive capacity of the economy. We are using the term, investment, here in a different way than you probably normally use the term. You probably use the term to refer to purchasing stock, bonds, insurance policies, and so forth. This type of investment is personal investment, which may have an important impact on your personal financial future, but which does not affect the productive capacity of the economy. When you buy so many shares of stock, somebody else is selling them. Thus, you have increased your investments, but this is canceled out by the fact that somebody else has decreased his or her investments. By contrast, when General Motors builds a new factory, and equips it with the necessary machines and tools to manufacture automobiles, the productive capacity of the economy is increased.

The amount of business spending on investment, during any given period, is largely dependent upon the availability of potentially profitable investment opportunities, and the cost and availability of investment funds. Let's look at each of these factors.

Availability of Investment Opportunities. There are a number of factors that determine the availability of profitable investment opportunities. Consumer demand is the most important of these factors. If manufacturers are unable to sell all of the products that they are currently capable of producing, there are no incentives for them to build new factories or buy additional machines.

Government tax policies also play an important role in determining the amount of investment that will take place. If business tax rates are high, businesses will have less after-tax profits, and thus less incentive to invest. However, if businesses are offered tax incentives to invest, they are more likely to increase their investment.

The invention of new products and the development of new technology often lead to large increases in business investment. Historically, periods of high investment have usually coincided with the development of new products and new technology. The invention of the automobile led to massive amounts of investment in factories, tools, and machines for the mass production of automobiles. More recently, the electronics industry, including computers, has provided good opportunities for new investment.

Since the invention of new products and the development of new industries is rather sporadic, good investment opportunities are more plentiful in some time periods than in others. Since investment spending is one of the three basic determinants of the level of GDP, fluctuations in investment can cause fluctuations in the GDP.

Cost and Availability of Investment Funds. Since much of the business investment that takes place is paid for with borrowed money, the availability of loans, and the interest rates that must be paid on these loans, are important determinants of the amount of investment that will take place during any given period of time. Both the savings rate and government policies are important in determining interest rates and the availability of loans.

Government Spending

Approximately 20 percent of the total spending is government spending. This includes the spending of federal, state, and local governments. Since government spending is a major determinant of the GDP, changes in government spending can have a substantial effect on GDP, and on inflation and unemployment. If the economy is operating at the full-employment level, with GDP growing so fast that increased inflation is likely, the government can attempt to reduce the danger of inflation by reducing government spending, and thus reducing the rate of growth of the GDP. On the other hand, if the economy is operating below the full-employment level, the government might increase spending in an effort to increase the level of GDP and reduce unemployment.

Equilibrium GDP

Equilibrium GDP occurs when the GDP is exactly equal to the level of total spending. In other words, the total spending for goods and services is exactly equal to the total production of goods and services, such that there is neither a shortage nor a surplus. In terms of supply and demand, consumer spending, plus investment spending, plus government spending is the total demand (aggregate demand) for goods and services. And GDP is the total supply (aggregate supply). Thus, at equilibrium GDP, total supply equals total demand. (Or, in the language of economists, aggregate supply equals aggregate demand at equilibrium GDP.) Since equilibrium is a point of rest, once GDP has reached the equilibrium level, there will be no tendency for it to change until total spending changes.

It is important to understand that equilibrium GDP is not always desirable. Equilibrium GDP simply means that GDP is remaining at its current level, and there is no tendency for it to change in either direction. Equilibrium GDP is good only if the current level of GDP is the most desirable level. It would be possible for the economy to be in equilibrium in the depths of a depression with millions of workers unemployed. Certainly this would not be a good equilibrium. In this case, we would want to implement policies that would increase the level of total spending and throw the GDP out of equilibrium, because during periods of high unemployment we want the GDP to be growing. Only when the economy reached the full-employment level with minimal inflation would we want GDP to be in equilibrium. In other words, the desired goal is for the GDP to be in equilibrium at the full-employment level, and only at the full-employment level.

Economic Growth

In addition to the goal of maintaining equilibrium GDP at the full employment level, another goal is to pursue policies that will enable the full-employment level of GDP to grow over time. In other words, we not only want our economy to produce as many goods and services as possible with our limited resources today, but we also want the capacity of the economy to grow so that we can produce still more goods and services in the future.

Economic growth is extremely important because, without it, there can be no improvements in the standard of living even if the size of the population remains constant. And, if the population grows at a time when we are not increasing the production of goods and services, the standard of living will actually decline.

The rate of economic growth depends primarily on the quantity and quality of productive resources (labor, natural resources, and capital goods), and on the efficiency with which these productive resources are used.

The United States has a highly skilled labor force, and an abundance of most natural resources, compared to many countries, although we do not have an inexhaustible supply. The United States also has a large supply of what economists call capital goods. **Capital goods**, which include such things as factories, machines, tools, railroads, trucks, and business buildings, are human-made resources that are used for the production of consumer goods and services, and additional capital goods. Without capital goods, natural resources are not very useful. Capital goods and labor are needed to turn the natural resources into the products the American people want.

The United States has concentrated much effort on the production of capital goods in the past, but it is necessary to continue to produce as many capital goods as possible if we want to maximize future economic growth. During periods when the economy is operating at full employment, the only way to increase the production of capital goods is to reduce the production of consumer goods temporarily. However, increased production of capital goods will increase the productive capacity of the economy and make possible the production of both more capital goods and more consumer goods in the future.

The efficiency with which labor is combined with the other productive resources determines labor productivity, which is an important determinant of economic growth. **Labor productivity** can be defined as the amount of output produced by a given quantity of labor. The more output we can get from our labor force, the greater will be the nation's economic growth. The quantity and quality of capital goods available to the labor force are important determinants of labor productivity.

CHAPTER 5

FISCAL POLICY AND FISCAL DISCIPLINE

Economists usually define fiscal policy as the deliberate use of the government's spending and taxing powers to influence economic activity. When the government raises or lowers taxes, or changes its spending levels, in order to bring about a desired change in the level of total spending, and thus the performance of the economy, it is practicing fiscal policy. Fiscal policy can also be defined more generally as simply the government's taxing and spending policies regardless of whether or not it is trying to bring about changes in the level of total spending in the economy.

Fiscal Policy in Theory

The origin of fiscal policy as a tool to bring about deliberate changes in the performance of the economy dates back to 1936 when a British economist, named John Maynard Keynes, published a monumental book, *The General Theory of Employment, Interest, and Money.* In this book, Keynes set forth a new economic theory that became known as **Keynesian economics.**

Keynesian economics soon became the predominant body of economic theory in the Western world. Although his theories have undergone substantial refinement and revision, much of modern Keynesian economics is still rooted on the ideas set forth by Keynes. Fiscal policy is a central part of Keynesian economics. Keynes argued that government should play an active role in maintaining the proper level of total spending in the economy in order to minimize both unemployment and inflation. He believed that, with the proper use of the government's spending and taxing powers, the extremes of the business cycle could be avoided.

The extremes of the business cycle, which result in high unemployment or high inflation, can be very costly. During a severe recession, millions of workers become unemployed, and billions of dollars worth of potential production are permanently lost. In addition, prolonged periods of high inflation can have a devastating effect on both the economy and the people.

The objectives of deliberate fiscal policy are to minimize unemployment and inflation by using the government's taxing and spending powers to assure the correct level of total spending, and thus the proper level of Gross Domestic Product. The principle determinant of the level of the Gross Domestic Product (GDP) is the level of total spending in the economy. Furthermore, if the GDP is too high, the economy will experience inflation, and if it is too low, the economy will suffer from unemployment. Therefore, in order to have a healthy economy, it is important to have the proper amount of total spending so the GDP will be neither too high nor too low.

Fiscal policy can be used to regulate the level of total spending. If total spending is too high, the government can lower its own spending and/or increase taxes so consumers will have less after-tax money to spend. If total spending is too low, the government can increase its own spending and/or reduce taxes, so consumers will have more after-tax money to spend. At least in theory, fiscal policy can be used to regulate the level of total spending, and thus the level of production. If GDP could be maintained at the appropriate level, it would be possible to avoid both high inflation and serious unemployment.

Fiscal Policy in Practice

Most mainstream economists believe that fiscal policy, if used properly, can be a strong tool for managing the economy. The best example of successful use of fiscal policy is the long period of economic expansion during the 1960s. When President John F. Kennedy took office in 1961, the economy was suffering from a recession that had begun in 1958. Kennedy brought into his administration economic advisers who were determined to use fiscal policy to bring the economy out of the recession. The first fiscal-policy measures included increased federal spending on highways, and legislation that allowed businesses to subtract from their taxes a part of the cost of new investment in factories and machines.

When these measures proved insufficient, the President proposed a major tax cut. Although President Kennedy was assassinated before the tax cut was enacted, his successor, Lyndon Johnson, signed an $11 billion tax cut into law in February 1964. This large tax cut, along with substantial increases in spending for the Vietnam War, fueled the longest economic expansion in American history. The expansion lasted from February 1961 to December 1969—106 consecutive months.

Probably few economists expected to see a repeat of the long expansion of the 1960s in their lifetime. However, at the time of this writing in June 2000, our economy is in the 111th consecutive month of the current expansion, which makes it the longest expansion ever. Although there will eventually be at least a mild recession to end the current sustained expansion, nobody knows when that will happen.

Fiscal policy does not have such a good track record in combating inflation, however. The problem is not that proper fiscal policies cannot successfully control inflation.

The problem is the political feasibility of getting the President and Congress to support the proper fiscal policies during periods of inflation. Many economists believe that when inflation began to rise in 1966, at a time of full employment, the government should have raised taxes and reduced government spending in order to lower the level of total spending and nip the inflation in the bud. But higher taxes and cuts in government programs are never popular with the public, and many politicians do not have the guts to do what is right for the economy because such unpopular actions might cost them votes in the next election.

If fiscal policy is to be used successfully for managing the economy, it must be possible to raise taxes as well as lower them, and to decrease government spending as well as increase it. If the general public and government officials had a clear understanding of basic economics, it might be possible to pursue sound fiscal policy in both controlling unemployment and inflation. But, as long as the majority of people cannot see how higher taxes will help to reduce inflation, it is unlikely that they will support the higher taxes when they are needed. Thus, fiscal policy is not very practical for fighting inflation.

Keynesian economics was the predominant body of economic theory for nearly half a century. Much of the content in the economics textbooks used at both the high school and college levels today is derived from Keynesian economics. And most mainstream economists are still strong supporters of the basic ideas set forth by Keynes and revised and refined by later Keynesian economists. In addition, prior to the Reagan administration, most government economic policies were based on Keynesian economics.

Supply-side Economics

In 1981, President Reagan abandoned Keynesian economics and launched the nation in a new direction based on a new, untested theory called *supply-side econom-*

ics. This new theory received most of its support from noneconomists. Only a small fraction of professionally-trained economists supported it. Usually, new economic theories require years of debate and testing before they stand a chance of being implemented as a part of government economic policy. But, because the ideas of the supply-side supporters were so compatible with the political philosophy of Ronald Reagan, this new, untested theory was to become the cornerstone of Reagan's economic policy.

The proponents of supply-side economics argued that taxes had risen to such a high level that they served to discourage work and investment. They contended that a sharp reduction in tax rates would provide strong incentives for workers to work harder and longer, and for businesses to produce more goods and services. The supply-side advocates argued that there would be so much additional work and production, as a result of the tax cut, that the government would actually collect more tax dollars than before, even with the lower tax rates. This was like having your cake and eating it too. According to supply-siders, the government could lower tax rates and at the same time collect more tax dollars.

In 1981, Congress enacted the president's tax-cut proposal. The proposal had been reduced, from a 30 percent cut to a 25 percent cut in personal income tax rates over a three-year period by Reagan's budget director. Although inflation did come down as the nation plunged into recession, the unemployment rate climbed to 10.7 percent in December 1982, the highest level since the Great Depression of the 1930s. And, instead of the promised balanced budget by 1984, the federal government ran an on-budget deficit of $185.7 billion in fiscal year 1984. In 1985 the on-budget deficit soared to $221.7 billion, and in 1986 it rose to $238.0 billion. The previous record on-budget deficit, prior to the Reagan presidency, was $72.7 billion in

1980. In 1970, just ten years before Reagan's election, the on-budget deficit was only $8.7 billion.

Although President Reagan abandoned Keynesian economics, Keynesian economics can be used to explain much of what happened during the Reagan presidency. First of all, the severe recession of 1981-82 that caused millions of Americans to lose their jobs might have been prevented. When President Reagan took office in January 1981, the economy was weak because it was still recovering from the mild recession that occurred during the Carter administration. In terms of fiscal policy, the economy needed a boost in the form of a substantial tax cut and/or increased government spending. If President Reagan had carried out his original plan to cut tax rates by 10 percent effective January 1981, the severe recession might have been avoided. But Budget Director, David Stockman, convinced the president to reduce his first year tax cut from 10 percent to 5 percent, and to delay its implementation from January 1 to October 1, 1981 in order to reduce the size of the deficit for that year.

Thus, instead of the planned 10 percent tax cut that was to have taken place in January 1981, there was no tax cut at all for the first 9 months of that year, and only a 5 percent cut for the last three months of the year. At the same time, the president was making substantial cuts in federal spending for domestic programs. The fragile economy simply could not stand the shock of such a stringent budget in 1981.

Budget Deficits

In January 1982, a full 10 percent cut in tax rates was added to the 5 percent cut of October 1981 and, in January 1983, the final 10 percent tax-rate cut took effect. Thus, effective January 1983, tax rates were 25 percent lower than just 15 months earlier. Some economists believe that if there had been a 10 percent cut in tax rates in January 1981, and no further cuts after that, the economic history of the 1980s might have been radically different. The nation might have avoided both the severe recession of 1981-82 and the huge budget deficits that sent the national debt soaring.

The 25 percent tax cut, implemented over a 15-month period between October 1981 and January 1983, was more medicine than the ailing economy could handle. The patient was harmed a great deal more than it was helped with this prescription. The large tax cut resulted in a substantial loss in revenue, and thus contributed to the gigantic budget deficits.

The huge tax cuts of 1982 and 1983 did help the economy to recover from the severe recession. There is no surer way to bring about a strong economic expansion than for the government to pump more than $200 billion more in spending into the economy than it takes out in the form of taxes as it did in 1983. The huge deficits made the strong recovery and expansion possible, but the nation paid a terrible price for this expansion. In a sense, we mortgaged our future.

The magnitude of the problems of the budget deficits, and the growth in the national debt, can be seen by examining Table 5-1, which presents data for selected years between 1960 and 2000. The federal government ran a very small on-budget surplus of $0.5 billion in 1960. However, in every other year between 1960 and 1999, the nation ran on-budget deficits.

The 1968 budget deficit of $27.7 billion during the Vietnam War was, at the time, the largest budget deficit since World War II. In 1976, 1980, and 1981, the government ran budget deficits in excess of $70 billion dollars, but during these periods the economy was in recession, and the deficits were due largely to the high unemployment that existed. When workers are laid off they stop paying income taxes, and the government begins to pay them unemployment compensation. This automatically increases the deficit.

TABLE 5-1: FEDERAL GOVERNMENT ON-
BUDGET DEFICITS AND NATIONAL DEBT FOR
SELECTED FISCAL YEARS 1960-1999
IN BILLIONS OF DOLLARS

Year	Surplus (+) or Deficit(-)	National Debt
1960	+0.5	290.5
1965	-1.6	322.3
1970	-8.7	380.9
1975	-55.3	541.9
1980	-72.7	909.1
1981	-74.0	994.8
1982	-120.1	1,137.3
1983	-208.0	1,371.7
1984	-185.7	1,564.7
1985	-221.7	1,817.5
1986	-238.0	2,120.6
1987	-169.3	2,346.1
1988	-194.0	2,601.3
1989	-205.2	2,868.0
1990	-277.8	3,206.6
1991	-321.6	3,598.5
1992	-340.5	4,002.1
1993	-300.5	4,351.4
1994	-258.9	4,643.7
1995	-226.4	4,921.0
1996	-174.1	5,181.9
1997	-103.4	5,369.7
1998	-30.0	5,478.7
1999	+0.7	5,606.1

Source: Economic Report of the President, 2000

According to Congressional Budget Office calculations, if the economy had been operating at the full-
employment level during these two years, there would have
been no deficits. It is in 1982 that the federal government

begins to run exceptionally large and sustained budget deficits on a regular year-by-year basis. In 1982, the deficit was $120.1 billion. The following year it soared to $208.0 billion. Although, the deficit fell slightly to $185.7 billion in 1984, it rose to $221.7 billion in 1985, and $238.0 billion in 1986. In 1987, with unemployment continuing to decline, the deficit fell to $169.3 billion. But the fiscal 1990 deficit was $277.8 billion, and by 1992 it had soared to $340.5 billion.

The large deficits of 1982, 1983, and 1984 can be attributed partly to the high unemployment resulting from the severe recession of 1981-82. However, the huge budget deficit of $221.7 billion in 1985 was at least partly caused by the excessive cuts in tax rates in 1982 and 1983. If we compare 1985 with 1980 (years with identical unemployment rates of 7.1 percent), we can see the basic change in the potential of the tax structure to generate sufficient revenue as a result of the cuts in tax rates. The 1980 deficit was only $72.7 billion, about one-third that of the enormous deficit of 1985.

Clearly, there was a basic structural problem with the federal budget. In the past, most deficits were due almost totally to unemployment. Thus, they were called cyclical deficits because they resulted from a downturn in the business cycle. When the economy again reached full employment, most of the deficit disappeared. However, by early 1990, the unemployment rate had fallen to its lowest level since the early 1970s, but large deficits remained. Only a small amount of the fiscal 1990 deficit was due to the unemployment rate. Most of the deficit was a structural deficit. The structural deficits resulted from the fact that the 25 percent cut in tax rates, during the early part of the Reagan presidency, created a situation where, even at full employment, the tax structure could not generate nearly enough revenue to provide a balanced budget.

The large deficits of the 1980s and early 1990s resulted in huge increases in the national debt. Every dollar that is spent by the government, above and beyond the amount of revenue it receives, must be borrowed. So each time the government borrows money to cover the deficit, this borrowed money is added to the national debt.

The Clinton Era

The economic policies of the Clinton administration represented a radical departure from those of the Reagan-Bush years. There was a return to more traditional economic policies, and the structural component of the budget deficit was at least partially eliminated with selective increases in income taxes combined with government spending cuts. The spending cuts, included some cuts in entitlement programs, and the collapse of the Soviet Union also allowed the United States government to make especially large cuts in defense spending. The budgetary policy reforms, along with the booming economy, permitted the deficit to be eliminated in 1999.

The National Debt

The national debt first reached the $1 trillion mark in 1981. It had taken the United States more than 200 years to accumulate this first $1 trillion of debt. However, it took just a little more than five years to add an additional $1 trillion, and thus double the national debt. In just five short years, the United States had added as much to the national debt as it had during the previous 200 years.

By 1990, the national debt had soared to more than $3 trillion, and by 1992 it had surpassed the $4 trillion mark. Between 1981 and 1992, the United States government quadrupled its national debt, and the debt surpassed the $5.6 trillion mark in 1999.

Although the nation is no longer running annual budget deficits, at least for the time being, the $4.6 trillion that we added to the debt during the past two decades will exist forever. Continuing to have balanced budgets in the future will do nothing to reduce the enormous debt that we have accumulated. Our children, grandchildren, and all the generations that follow them, will have to pay interest on this enormous debt forever. And each additional dollar that must go to pay for interest on the national debt is one less dollar available for education, health programs, national defense, or tax relief. If interest rates should soar to record levels in the future, as they have in the past, the government would have to pay the high interest rates just like everyone else. This could mean drastic cuts in government services.

Our nation cannot afford to spend beyond its means in the years ahead. There is little that can be done about past deficits and growth in the national debt, but we dare not return to the policy of paying for today's government with tomorrow's money. In the past, when the United States ran budget deficits, most of the money to finance the deficits was borrowed from Americans. This meant that whenever interest was paid on the debt, it was paid to Americans and went right back into the nation's economy.

However, the gigantic budget deficits of the past two decades made it impossible for the U.S. Government to totally finance its deficits by borrowing only from the nation's citizens. Americans generate just about enough savings to cover loans needed by consumers and businesses. So there are not nearly enough funds to finance the federal deficits, in addition to meeting the demands for loans by the private sector of the economy. Thus, the United States has borrowed increasing amounts from foreign sources in recent years. As a result, during the 1980s, the United States was transformed from the world's largest lender to the world's largest borrower.

Balancing the Budget
Now that the annual deficit problem has been brought under control, how should the economy be managed in the future to prevent a recurrence of the experience of the past? Should we have a policy of balancing the

budget each and every year? Many people think so, and some even want a constitutional amendment that would require an annually balanced budget. People who think in these terms do not have a clear understanding of how the economy works. Most economists favor balancing the budget under the right circumstances, but few economists support the idea of a balanced budget each and every year. There are basically three alternative balanced-budget policies: the annually balanced budget; the cyclically balanced budget; and the full-employment balanced budget.

An **annually balanced budget** would be one where total government revenue is exactly equal to total government expenditures each and every year. Although an annually balanced budget may seem attractive in theory, few economists would support such a policy.

Since most of the federal government's revenue comes from the individual and corporate income taxes, the government's revenue is very much influenced by the business cycle. During periods of recession, when unemployment is high and many corporations are losing money instead of making profits, government revenue falls off sharply. At the same time, government expenditures for unemployment compensation and other social programs rises in response to the increased unemployment. The combined effect of reduced tax revenue and increased spending will inevitably lead to a larger budget deficit.

If the government attempted to balance the budget during a severe recession by increasing taxes and/or reducing government spending, the resulting decline in total spending would lead to still more unemployment and an even larger deficit. Raising taxes and/or reducing government spending during a period of high unemployment will cause still more workers to lose their jobs. As this happens, the newly unemployed workers will stop paying income taxes and will begin receiving unemployment compensation payments from the government. Thus, the deficit will be driven still higher. It is inevitable that the nation will experience budget deficits during periods of recession and high unemployment. The only way to reduce these deficits is to pursue policies that will restore full employment to the economy. Therefore, an annually balanced budget is not feasible.

With a **cyclically balanced budget**, the government would attempt to balance the budget over the course of the business cycle. During periods of recession, there would be deficits because of the loss of tax revenue from unemployed workers and the increased spending for such programs as unemployment compensation. However, as the economy recovered from a recession, the government would receive additional tax dollars from the newly employed workers who are recalled to their jobs and would spend decreasing amounts on unemployment compensation and similar programs. The net result would be a decline in the deficit.

On the other hand, during periods of economic prosperity, when total spending is so high that it threatens to increase the inflation rate, the government would spend less than it collected in taxes, thus creating budget surpluses. Under such a policy, during some years there would be balanced budgets, during other years there would be deficits, and during still other years there would be a surplus in the budget. If the surpluses offset the deficits, over a period of years, total government spending would be approximately equal to total revenue, and thus, there would be a balanced budget over the long run.

The cyclically balanced budget is a far sounder budget policy than the annually balanced budget, and it is much closer to the way family budgets operate. Very few families operate on an annually balanced budget every year throughout their entire lives. Usually, when a young couple gets married and begins a family, they run deficits for the first several years of their married life. They borrow money to buy such things as a car, a home, and furniture. When they purchase these items, they are spending far more than they are earning, so they are running budget deficits. However, after a period of 20 or more years, the home mortgage and other loans should be paid off. At this point, a wise couple will begin saving toward retirement. Therefore, for many years they will be spending less than they earn which will result in surpluses in their budget to offset the deficits of earlier years.

Once they retire, most families will again begin running deficits in the sense that they are now living off the surpluses they built up over the years when they were saving for retirement. At the end of their lives, most couples will have spent just about as much as they have earned, thus balancing their budgets over a lifetime. Some will have accumulated a surplus that they will leave behind as inheritance for their children, and still others will leave debts behind, meaning they have spent more during their lifetimes than they have earned.

In theory, a cyclically balanced budget would help to even out the high and low points of the business cycle and, at the same time, lead to a balanced budget over the long run. However, in actual practice, the results would probably be different. Since the business cycles are not uniform or predictable, it would be highly unlikely that the surpluses and deficits would exactly cancel one another out in any given time period.

The other budget alternative is the **full-employment balanced (or surplus) budget**. Under this policy, the federal budget would be balanced when, and only when, the economy is approaching the full-employment level. The government would estimate the total revenue that it would receive when the economy was operating at the full-employment level. The budget would then be structured so that spending would be equal to revenue when the economy was slightly below the full-employment level. When the economy reached the full-employment level, there would be a surplus in the budget. But, if the economy slipped into a recession, there would be a decline in tax revenue, an increase in government spending for unemployment compensation, and a budget deficit.

This is the budget policy that is probably supported by the largest number of economists. Almost all economists believe the government should have a balanced budget or a surplus when the economy is operating at the full-employment level. But, when the economy is operating below the full-employment level, it is necessary for the government to put more money into the economy in spending than it takes out in taxes.

During recession, the deficit is actually beneficial to the economy because the excess government expenditure, relative to the amount of tax revenue collected, will help the economy to recover from the recession. When the economy has recovered from the recession and is once again approaching the full-employment level, the deficit will disappear. When the economy actually reaches the full-employment level, there should be a budget surplus. If the budget is structured so there will be a surplus at the full-employment level, the surpluses might approximately offset the deficits so that an approximately balanced budget could be attained over a period of several years.

In summary, a nation cannot continue to have large budget deficits year after year, indefinitely. The United States government lived beyond its means for a long time, but the time of reckoning came. Our nation closed the gap between revenue and expenditures in its operating budget (excluding Social Security) during the 1999 fiscal year and must pursue a policy of attempting to balance the budget over the long run in future years. It is absolutely irresponsible to even consider major increases in government spending, or major tax cuts, until and unless we pay back at least a portion of the $4.6 trillion that our government has borrowed over the past 20 years.

CHAPTER 6

VOODOO ECONOMICS

As stated earlier, for purposes of this book I am using the term "voodoo economics" as a synonym for economic malpractice. Economic malpractice occurs when policy makers pursue economic practices and policies that are not consistent with sound economic principles, as viewed by the majority of professionally-trained economists, and when such unsound practices inflict damage on the economy.

In the medical field, when doctors take actions that are not consistent with what the majority of doctors consider to be sound medicine, and when such actions result in injury to the patient, the patient is entitled to sue the doctor for damages resulting from the malpractice. Doctors are not entitled to experiment with their patients. They must stick to medical treatments that have proven effective in the past, and which are generally supported by the majority of medical professionals. Doctors who deliberately deviate from these standards may loose their medical license to practice and may be ordered to pay millions of dollars in damages by the courts.

If a would-be doctor who has never been to medical school were to risk the life of a patient by performing surgery on the patient, that would-be doctor would end up behind bars. Yet, during the early years of the Reagan administration radical experimental surgery was performed on the American economy, which adversely affected millions of people, by government officials who had little knowledge of economics. These actions were taken despite the fact that the majority of professionally trained economists did not support them, and they were implemented over the protests of Nobel-prize-winning economists.

Economic Illiteracy and Voodoo Economics
When a medical doctor steps outside the bounds of traditional and conventional medicine (by endorsing and supporting doctor-assisted suicide, for example), it becomes a worldwide news story. This results in widespread public debate and sometimes actions to stop the nontraditional practice of medicine. However, when government policy makers take actions that are detrimental to the long-term health of the economy in order to practice what appears to be good short-term politics, the public is rarely made aware of these actions by the news media.

It's not that journalists have no interest in reporting economic malpractice. The problem is that most journalists would not recognize economic malpractice if it were staring them in the face. Once again, this is not the fault of journalists. It is the fault of the American educational system. Most journalists have had little or no formal instruction in economics just as the majority of Americans in most fields have received little or no formal education in the field of economics.

This widespread economic illiteracy poses one of the greatest threats to America's future, and it is the primary cause of all past voodoo economics. It is also the reason for the political popularity of current voodoo-economics proposals by both presidential candidates. Economic illiteracy threatens our future, both as individuals and as a nation. This major national problem is evidenced by the following excerpt from the June 14, 1999 issue of *U.S. News & World Report.*

"On a recent nationwide test of basic economic principles, two thirds of the 1,085 high school students who took it did not even know that the stock market is where people buy and sell shares—never mind that investments can tumble. Worse, few understood that scarcity drives up prices or that money loses value in times of inflation—two consumer fundamentals. Average grade: F"

The magazine article refers to a study conducted by Louis Harris & Associates on behalf of the National Council on Economic Education. The survey is based on interviews with a national cross-section of 1,010 adults aged 18 and over and a representative sample of 1,085 students in grades 9 through 12.

The results of the survey are shocking. On average, adults got a grade of 57 percent for their knowledge of basic economics compared to an average score of only 48 percent for high school students. Specifically, only 37 percent of adults and 36 percent of students recognized that the statement, "money holds its value well in times of inflation" is incorrect. In the area of public finance, only 54 percent of adults and 23 percent of high school students knew that when the federal government spends more in a year than it collects in revenue for that year, there is a budget deficit. Also, 22 percent of adults and 25 percent of students confuse the definition of a budget deficit with the national debt.

The National Council on Economic Education, who commissioned the national survey of economic literacy, is a nonprofit partnership of leaders in education, business, and labor. The council has established a nationwide network of state councils and over 260 university-based centers to train teachers to teach economics to our nation's young people. One week after releasing the shocking results of its national survey on economic literacy, the Council announced an ambitious five-year, nationwide campaign to increase economic literacy among both students and adults.

"Despite the failing grades and the revelation that only 13 states require students to take a course in economics before graduation, the research also told us that a resounding 96 percent of Americans want basic economics taught in our schools," stated Robert Duvall, President and CEO of the Council. "We intend to be the catalyst to make that happen. As of today, we are mounting a concerted drive to focus national attention on the need to make economics an educational priority for every American."

Although economics has a greater impact on our daily lives than almost any other academic subject, most high school graduates are never exposed to the subject. In addition, most college graduates have not taken a single course in economics. All high school students are required to study American History and American Government presumably so they will be "better citizens" and "better-informed" voters. This is good, but it is impossible to have a clear understanding of either United States History or American Government without a clear understanding of basic economic principles and a knowledge of how the American Economy operates.

It is difficult to make sense out of the fact that only 13 states require students to take a course in economics before graduation. It should become a top priority of every high school in America to add a course in economics to their curriculum if they don't already have one.

The Mystery of Economics

Most Americans have almost no understanding of the field of economics. They know the basics of American history and have at least some understanding of American government. But the field of economics, which affects their lives more than any other subject, is as foreign to them as Latin. Even worse, some people who know nothing about economics seem to think they know everything.

Economic illiteracy is one of America's greatest threats. It has played a leading role in the practice of voodoo economics in the past, and it is the primary reason that most Americans believe the hoax that the nation has a huge budget surplus as many top politicians are claiming.

Most members of Congress and other top government officials would probably fail a general test on economic literacy. Most have never had a course in economics, but still think they know enough about the subject to pass judgment on which economic proposals are sound and which are not. This has gotten the nation into great trouble in the past and will continue to do so in the future.

The primary problem is that many people, including members of Congress and other top government officials, know very little about economics but think they know a great deal. They have an extremely simplistic notion of what economics is about and believe that they are capable of making decisions about it without consulting experts. Many have the mistaken notion that economics is a business subject. It is not. It is a highly complex social science.

Economics can be defined as *the study of how individuals and society choose to use limited resources in an effort to satisfy people's unlimited wants.* But there is so much more to it than this simplified definition suggests. There are some elements of common sense in the study of economics but, overall, economics is a highly sophisticated science. The following short excerpt from the article on economics in *Encyclopedia Americana* is a good summary of the scientific nature of the field of economics.

> "Like medicine or engineering, economics is a rigorous discipline. Hard thinking has produced hypotheses, and those hypotheses have been tested by empirical observation and, where possible, by careful measurement. When the results turned out to be inconsistent with the hypotheses, more hard thinking came up with new hypotheses. The method of economics, then, is not different from the methods of other sciences."

Economics is one of the six categories in which the coveted Nobel prize is awarded to persons "who have made outstanding contributions for the benefit of mankind." The other five categories are, medicine, physics, chemistry, literature, and peace.

Congress would never consider enacting legislation on medicine, physics, or chemistry, without considering the views of experts in these fields. Yet, during the Reagan administration, Budget Director David Stockman, who had never had even an introductory course in the field of economics, became the chief architect of economic policy and totally ignored and defied the warnings of outstanding professional economists some of whom had been awarded the Nobel Prize.

America paid an enormous price for that economic malpractice. Yet, at the time of this writing, it appears that the American people may elect a new president who is expounding proposals, including a major tax cut, that are totally contrary to the thinking of most mainstream professional economists. Most Americans, including top government officials, do not know much more about economics than they know about chemistry or physics. However, they are aware that they don't know much about chemistry or physics, but unaware that they are equally illiterate in the field of economics.

The Role of Government in the American Economy

Absolutely everything the government does affects the economy in some way either positively or negatively. So whether or not the government is trying to have an impact on the economy when it takes certain actions, we can be sure that the actions will have some effect on the economy. In the field of medicine, doctors know that treating a patient for one medical problem could result in bad side effects and make another problem even worse. Extensive research has been done in an effort to determine what potential side effects can occur as a result of any given course of treatment, and doctors exercise great caution in an effort to avoid harming the patient in some other way when they treat him or her for any particular condition.

There are many economic side effects to all major government actions even when the government has no desire to have an impact on the economy. This is why a careful analysis of any proposed action should be made by competent professionally trained economists before the action is taken, and the findings of the economists should be taken into consideration by policy makers.

It is especially critical to note that any increase or decrease in government spending and any increase or decrease in taxes will have a significant impact on the performance of the economy. The nature of this impact will depend upon the stage of the business cycle in which the economy is currently operating. If the economy is in a severe recession with high unemployment, either an increase in government spending or a decrease in taxes will have a positive effect on the economy.

The additional purchase of goods and services resulting from a direct increase in government spending, and the increased consumer spending resulting from the additional "take-home" pay following a tax cut, will increase total spending (aggregate demand) and thus help the economy to recover from the recession. Thus, in times of recession and high unemployment, any actions that result in an increase in aggregate demand will have a positive impact on the performance of the economy.

However, at a time when the economy is at the peak of the business cycle, with very low unemployment and labor shortages, an increase in government spending or a decrease in taxes is just about the worst thing the government could do. Yet, at the time of this writing, one presidential candidate is proposing increased spending, and the other candidate is proposing a major tax cut. This is at a time when the Fed has been raising interest rates month after month in order to slow the economy down to a sustainable rate of growth. Any substantial increase in aggregate demand at this time would nullify the efforts of the Fed to slow down the economy. In addition, it would likely lead to a surge in inflation, and then lead to an abrupt halt to the expansion and a plunging of the economy into a recession.

Do Al Gore and George W. Bush have so little understanding of basic economics that they don't realize the disastrous nature of their proposals? Have they not discussed the effects of their economic proposals with highly competent economists? Or, do they realize that their proposals are unsound but are advocating them anyway for political reasons?

The potential damage to the economy from Gore's proposals are not yet clear because we do not know enough specifics of what Gore plans to do. He has proposed using at least some of the alleged surplus for debt reduction, which is sound economics. However, he also seems to have plans for additional domestic spending. By the time this book is published, the positions of the two candidates will be much clearer, and readers can judge for themselves whether Gore's proposals involve the same degree of economic malpractice as Bush's proposal for major tax cuts. If Gore proposes increasing government spending by as much as Bush's proposed tax cut, then Gore's plan is just as economically unsound as Bush's plan.

The potential damage from George W. Bush's plan for a major tax cut is not in doubt. And the likelihood that Bush will change his position before election day is remote. His proposed tax cut is the centerpiece of his campaign, and his supporters would feel betrayed if he reneged. But he must change his position for the good of the nation even if he waits until after he is elected (if he is elected) to withdraw the tax cut proposal.

A major tax cut at this time would be one of the most damaging and irresponsible acts that any president could take. In addition to derailing the economy because of excess aggregate demand, it would lead to more large budget deficits in the years ahead and a new round of acceleration in the already gigantic national debt. The tax structure is already insufficient to balance the budget except in occasional years when the unemployment rate is extremely low. Additional tax cuts would further diminish the capacity of the tax structure to generate enough revenue to offset even stringent government spending measures.

Bush and his supporters seem to be focusing almost entirely on the "desirability" of a tax cut. Of course, everyone would like to have a tax cut if the government truly had the money to finance one, and if the economy were in a stage of the business cycle where the cut would help the economy instead of hurting it. But neither of these conditions exists. Bush has frequently said, "The surplus money in the government budget belongs to the people—not to the government—and it should be returned to the people." That is a hard argument to resist, but the statement is not true. The surplus in the Social Security Trust Fund which exists because, and only because, of the 1983 legislation which raised social security taxes in order to build up a surplus before the retirement of the baby boomers, belongs neither to the government nor to the people at large. It belongs to the Trust Fund and to the people who have paid Social Security taxes into it. To take money from the Social Security cookie jar and put it mostly on the plates of the very rich seems to me to be unfair and unethical in addition to being damaging to the American economy.

Voodoo Economics Prior to Reaganomics
Probably the first time that any administration was even a little guilty of economic malpractice was during the Great Depression. However, it is hard to hold Hoover responsible because modern economic science was still in its infancy. And, although Roosevelt was slow to take the correct actions, he did gradually implement fairly sound economic policies.

During the late 1920s, the economy was strong and prosperous. However, during the Great Depression of the 1930s, the nation suffered enormous poverty and suffering. The unemployment rate reached 25 percent, and millions of Americans were hungry and homeless. Yet, at a time when men, women, and children picked through garbage in search of food, sheep raisers in the western states slaughtered sheep by the thousands and destroyed their carcasses. The market price for sheep had fallen below the cost of shipping them to market so that farmers would lose money if they shipped their sheep to market. And while millions of Americans were without bread, wheat was left in the fields uncut because the price of wheat was too low to cover the harvesting costs.

In addition, many of the nation's factories, that could have been turning out goods, and providing the jobs, that Americans wanted and needed so desperately, sat partially or totally idle. The factories did not operate because they couldn't sell their products, and people couldn't buy the products because they didn't have jobs. The American economic system was simply allowed to break down, and it remained broken down for a decade.

The cost of the Great Depression was astronomical. According to estimates by economic historians, if the economy had fully used all of its resources during the 1930s, the dollar value of the additional production would have been higher than the cost of World War II. This would have been enough money to have covered the cost of a new house, and several new cars, for every American family during the decade.

The real tragedy is that the Great Depression never really needed to happen. The nation had all the productive resources necessary to produce a prosperous lifestyle during the 1930s just as it did in the 1920s. However, many of the resources were allowed to remain idle while millions were hungry and homeless. The policy makers of the

1930s can, however, be excused to some degree because modern economics was still young and untested.

After winning the election, Roosevelt continued to follow many of the same economic policies as Hoover at first. However, he gradually began to adopt some of the principles of modern economics that had been introduced by British economist, John Maynard Keynes. In 1935, Keynes published a monumental book, *The General Theory of Employment, Interest, and Money.* In this book, Keynes set forth a new economic theory that became known as Keynesian economics.

Keynesian economics soon became the predominant body of economic theory in the Western world. Keynes came to the United States and met with President Roosevelt in an effort to persuade him to use the new economic knowledge to bring the economy out of the depression. Roosevelt reportedly told an aide after Professor Keynes left that he didn't understand what Keynes had said. Keynes allegedly then took out a full page ad in the New York Times in which he wrote an open letter to the President of the United States, once again explaining what steps needed to be taken to get the economy out of the depression.

Roosevelt gradually became a convert to the new economic thinking and began pursuing policies, including public-employment programs, that would stimulate aggregate demand and put the unemployed back to work. The economy did improve, but Roosevelt and the Congress were not willing to provide a strong enough dose of medicine to truly get the economy back on track. It was the massive spending on World War II that returned the economy to prosperity.

It is extremely important to note that it was not the war itself, but the spending on the war that provided sufficient aggregate demand to return the economy to full employment. If there had never been a war, but the government had spent as much as it did on the war on other projects such as building roads, schools, hospitals, and so forth, the economy could have shown the same healthy economic growth that it did as a result of spending on the war.

The Employment Act of 1946

As the war came to an end, there was much fear that the economy would slip right back into the depression without the war expenditures. In an effort to do everything possible to keep this from happening, Congress passed the Employment Act of 1946. This act pledged the commitment of the United States government to provide "conditions under which there will be afforded useful employment opportunities, including self-employment, for those able, willing, and seeking to work, and to promote maximum employment, production, and purchasing power."

As part of the Act, Congress set up a Council of Economic Advisers to the President and required the President to send an annual economic report to the Congress, describing the state of the economy and suggesting improvements. Under this legislation, the President is mandated to select a Council of Economic Advisers so that he will always have access to trained professional economists who theoretically would guide the President away from potential economic malpractice.

The problem is that some past presidents have totally ignored the advice of their own economic advisers and deliberately engaged in economic malpractice. President Lyndon B. Johnson was the first president to flagrantly violate the intent of the Employment Act of 1946 by turning his back on the sound economic advice of his economic advisers and listening instead to his political advisers.

President Johnson's economic advisers urged him to raise taxes to offset the substantial increase in military expenditures on the Vietnam War. They warned that failure to do so could set off a prolonged period of high inflation. However, Johnson's political advisers told him that to do so would not be good politics. They suggested that to tell the American people that they were going to have to pay more taxes because of the war would be the equivalent of political suicide. At this time, the war was becoming increasingly unpopular with the people, so they would be especially irritated at the prospects of paying higher taxes for the war. Johnson believed that raising taxes would prevent him from being elected to another term, and so he placed personal political considerations above pursuing sound economic policies. Later, when political polls indicated that Johnson was not likely to get re-elected under any circumstances, he announced that he had decided not to seek re-election. It was at this time that Johnson called on Congress to enact a small temporary tax increase to head off inflation. A temporary 10 percent surtax was finally enacted in 1968 but it was more than two years too late to nip the inflationary pressures in the bud.

America paid an incredible price for President Johnson's failure to listen to the advice of his own hand-picked Council of Economic Advisers. In 1965, the economy was in one of the best positions ever. The unemployment rate was 4.5 percent, the inflation rate was 1.6 percent, and the government ran a budget deficit of only $1.4 billion. This was the seventh year in a row that the inflation rate had remained below 2 percent, and the unemployment rate was at its lowest level in 8 years. The federal budget was almost in balance, and the nation exported more goods than it imported. And then we blew it!

The first major economic policy error was the failure of the government to curb the excess demand for goods and services during the late sixties. The escalation of the Vietnam War in 1966 led to a substantial unplanned increase in military expenditures. The large increase in government spending caused total spending to rise above the full-employment capacity of the economy. With total spending exceeding the capacity of the economy to produce, prices began to rise and the nation embarked on a long journey of demand-pull inflation.

Although it is easy to blame the Vietnam War for the inflation, it was not the war but the financing of the war that caused the inflationary problems. When military spending was escalated in 1966, the economy was operating at the lowest level of unemployment—3.8 percent—in thirteen years. Not since 1953 had the unemployment rate dropped below 4 percent. Thus, the economy was operating near its maximum capacity output, and any increase in any component of total spending would have to be offset by an equal decrease elsewhere or demand-pull inflation would occur. If the government demanded an increase in the production of military goods, there would have to be a corresponding decrease in the production of domestic goods. And any decrease in the production of consumer goods would have to be matched by an equal decrease in consumer spending if rising prices were to be averted.

Thus, President Johnson's economic advisers argued for a tax increase to finance the increased military spending. Not only would the tax increase help to avoid deficits in the federal budget at a time of full employment, but it would also reduce the disposable income of consumers and curtail their level of spending. A tax increase was just what the economy needed in order to avoid major inflation, but President Johnson was very reluctant to call for a tax increase to finance an increasingly unpopular war.

When the President was finally convinced that a tax increase was absolutely necessary, Congress began to drag its feet. Thus, there was a delay of more than two years in getting the much-needed tax increase. By the time that it was finally implemented, inflation was too far out of control to be stopped by the small tax increase. During the three years, 1966, 1967, and 1968, the federal government ran deficits totaling $37.7 billion. The economy was operating at full capacity, and thus was not capable of any significant increase in the production of goods and services.

Yet the government pumped $37.7 billion more into the economy in the form of spending than it took out in the form of taxes during this three-year period. This huge increase in purchasing power, which could not be matched by a similar increase in supply of goods and services, could only lead to rising prices.

After seven years with inflation rates below two percent, the inflation rate rose to 2.9 percent in 1966, 4.2 percent in 1968, and 5.5 percent in 1969. The inflation was to get much worse during the 1970s and 1980s—11.0 percent in 1974, and 13.5 percent in 1980. Although much of the inflation of the 1970s resulted from the energy crises and soaring prices for crude oil, these special problems just added to the inflationary pressures started in the 1960s when the government failed to raise taxes in time to prevent the increased spending on the Vietnam War from setting off a prolonged period of demand-pull inflation.

Although the name had not yet been invented, President Lyndon B. Johnson was clearly the first president to engage in voodoo economics. It took sixteen years and the most severe economic downturn since the Great Depression (the 1981-82 recession) to break the back of the inflationary pressures set off by the economic malpractice during the Johnson years.

In summary, economic illiteracy is one of the greatest threats to the future of the American economy. Because of widespread economic illiteracy, it is possible for politicians to engage in major economic malpractice without being held accountable by the voters. And America has suffered a great deal because of that economic malpractice.

The Great Depression of the 1930s demonstrates just how big a price the nation can pay for failure to follow sound economic policies. However, since modern economics was still young and untested in the 1930s, political leaders of that period can be excused on the basis that they did not really know very much about the economy.

The economic malpractice during the Johnson administration is an entirely different matter as is that during the Reagan years. Both President Johnson and President Reagan ignored the advice of their own economic advisers in order to pursue political goals. America paid a terrible price, and millions of Americans suffered needlessly because of the failure of President Johnson and President Reagan to follow sound economic policies. The American people should demand that all future presidents take into consideration the advice of professional economists when making major decisions involving the economy.

CHAPTER 7

VOODOO ECONOMICS
DURING THE REAGAN-BUSH YEARS

In 1981, President Reagan abandoned Keynesian economics, which had been the predominant body of economic theory for nearly half a century, and launched the nation in a new direction based on a new, untested theory called supply-side economics. This new theory, which received most of its support from politicians and other non-economists, had the support of only a very few professionally-trained economists.

Usually, new economic theories require years of debate and testing before they stand a chance of being implemented as a part of government economic policy even when they are the product of some of the greatest minds in the field. But, because the ideas of the supply-side supporters were so compatible with the political philosophy of Ronald Reagan, the new, untested theory was to become the cornerstone of Reagan's economic policy.

The Origins of Supply-side Economics
Most professional economists had probably never heard the term "supply-side economics" until Ronald Reagan announced his support for it in the 1980 primary campaign. I had a Ph.D. degree in economics and had been teaching the subject to college students for more than a

dozen years at the time Reagan introduced the concept to the world. Yet, I had never seen any reference to the concept in any of the professional literature, and it was not included in any textbook that I had ever used.

There is good reason for this. The theory almost came out of nowhere. Robert Merry and Kenneth Bacon stated in a February 18, 1981 *Wall Street Journal* article, "Capturing the Executive Branch of government was an amazing victory for the supply-side movement, which hardly existed a mere eight years ago." And so it was. Never before had an economic theory so new, so untested, and with so little support from professional economists as a whole, been accepted and pushed by the federal government.

According to Merry and Bacon, supply-side economics became a political movement when the ideas of Arthur Laffer of the University of Southern California, and Robert Mundell of Columbia, captured the imagination of Jude Wanniski, an editorial writer for the *Wall Street Journal,* who reportedly sought receptive Washington politicians and finally found one in Representative Jack Kemp of New York. In 1977, Representative Kemp, along with Senator William Roth of Delaware, coauthored the Kemp-Roth Bill to slash individual income tax rates by 30 percent over a three-year period. Mr. Kemp then reportedly set out to convert Mr. Reagan, whom he considered the most receptive of the potential presidents.

The ideas and objectives of the supply-siders were very compatible with Mr. Reagan's own political philosophy, so it was not difficult to convert him to the new economic theories. Thus, Reagan's pledge to support passage of the Kemp-Roth Bill and call for a 30 percent cut in tax rates over a three-year period became the most popular promise of his campaign and undoubtedly played a major role in his big win.

Supply-side economists emphasized the interrelationship between the total supply of goods and services and the government's taxing and spending policies. They believed that tax rates had become so high that there was a disincentive to work or produce. Some also argued that subsidies to the poor were so generous that they discouraged the poor from increasing their earnings for fear their government aid would be reduced.

President Reagan's proposed 30 percent cut in tax rates over a three-year period was based on the argument that such a tax cut would result in a substantial increase in the total supply of goods and services produced. The argument was based on the belief that tax rates were so high that many individuals took more lengthy vacations, accepted less overtime work, and retired earlier than they would if tax rates were substantially lower. In addition, the supply-siders argued that the high tax rates discouraged business people from pursuing promising but risky investment opportunities because even if they were successful the government would take much of the profits in higher taxes.

These beliefs led supply-siders to argue that a massive tax cut, such as Reagan's proposal for a 30 percent cut in tax rates over a three-year period, would lead to more revenue, not less. Here is where the theories left the real world and entered fantasyland. The American people were being told that they could have their cake and eat it too, and they loved it. According to Reagan, he could cut tax rates by 30 percent and collect more revenue than before the tax cut. In fact, President Reagan promised that if Congress would just enact his proposal, the federal budget would be balanced by 1984 and he would simultaneously reduce both unemployment and inflation.

The Results of Supply-side Economics

The Congress did enact the President's economic program, including the tax-cut proposal, which had been reduced (at the request of Budget Director David Stockman) from a 30 percent cut to a 25 percent cut in personal income tax rates over a three-year period.   However, the country soon learned that the promised simultaneous reduction in inflation and unemployment rates was not to be.   Inflation did come down, as the economy plunged into the worst recession in half a century.   The civilian unemployment rate climbed to 10.7 percent in December 1982, the highest since the Great Depression of the 1930s. Millions of Americans lost their jobs, and the annual civilian unemployment rate remained above 9.5 percent for both 1982 and 1983.

As the economy recovered from the severe recession, President Reagan argued that his economic   policies were working and the economy was headed toward true and lasting prosperity.   On the surface things did look encouraging. The unemployment rate was gradually declining, and inflation was remaining low. However, a huge cloud hung over the optimism because of the unprecedented size of the federal budget deficits and the rapid growth in the national debt.

A president who had promised that his policies would lead to a balanced budget by 1984, instead gave us record budget deficits and a doubling of the national debt in six years. The Reagan administration added more to the national debt in six years than all the other presidents combined, from George Washington through Jimmy Carter, had added in more than 200 years. The federal budget deficits soared from $73.8 billion in fiscal 1980 to a record $221.2 billion in fiscal 1986.

Nations, like individuals, cannot indefinitely live beyond their means. While much of the borrowed money came from Americans who invested in government securities, substantial amounts of foreign capital was used to finance the huge budget deficits.   Between 1981 and 1986, the United States was transformed from the world's largest lender to the world's largest borrower.

What Went Wrong?

Why were the basic economic problems allowed to grow to such disastrous proportions? The primary reason was that for the first time in modern history, an American president chose to almost totally ignore the advice of professional economists, both inside and outside of the administration. Unless an economist could be found whose advice was compatible with Reaganomics, the administration simply ignored the advice. It would have been bad enough if the President had just ignored the advice of outside economists and had listened to his own handpicked economists. However, he ignored both groups.

President Reagan was required to appoint a Council of Economic Advisers to meet the legal requirement of the Employment Act of 1946. One of the provisions of this act required the President to appoint a Council of Economic Advisers so that he would always have close access to the advice of some of the best professional economists in the country. Thus, President Reagan did appoint three economists to his Council of Economic Advisers. Unfortunately, however, he chose not to listen to their advice and allowed people with little or no professional training in economics to formulate his economic policies.

When Murray Weidenbaum, Reagan's first Chairman of the Council of Economic Advisers, resigned early in the administration, the President had the opportunity to search the nation for his type of economist as Weidenbaum's replacement. Finally, in 1982, he selected Martin Feldstein, a Harvard economist, as his new Chairman.

Mr. Feldstein took his appointment seriously, and he expected to influence economic policy within the administration. He immediately began to warn the President about the gigantic federal budget deficits and insisted that something be done to reduce them. However, Feldstein soon learned that he had been appointed only to fill the position, and that his advice was not going to be taken seriously.

When Feldstein warned of the deficit dangers in the annual Economic Report of the President, Treasury Secretary, Donald Reagan, a noneconomist who was playing a major role in economic policy making, told Congress, "As far as I'm concerned, you can throw it (The Economic Report) away." Feldstein had warned that the deficits, if not curtailed soon, could devastate the nation's economy. Feldstein had argued that taxes should be raised as a way of reducing the projected $180 billion fiscal 1985 deficit. (As it turned out the actual on-budget deficit for fiscal 1985 was $212.7 billion.)

Earlier, in 1983, Feldstein had said, "If Congress doesn't act soon to cut future deficits, interest rates will remain high and weaken the economy. Future back-to-back $200 billion deficits will increase the national debt by an additional $1 trillion over the next few years, eventually forcing the government to implement drastic spending cuts and tax increases."

When Feldstein, out of frustration, began giving public speeches on the subject of the dangerous deficits, he was ordered to submit his speeches to the White House for prior approval before giving them. The final straw fell when, just a short time before Feldstein was scheduled to appear on an ABC news show on Sunday February 5, 1984, he was ordered by the White House to cancel the scheduled appearance because his comments might embarrass   the administration.

When Feldstein left the administration in 1984, President Reagan proposed abolishing the Council of Economic Advisers because he felt it served no useful purpose. When Congress created the Council of Economic Advisers with the Employment Act of 1946, the main concern was that all future presidents have close access to the best professionally trained economists available in order to avoid major economic policy mistakes. President Reagan, who had demonstrated repeatedly throughout his administration through his speeches and actions that he had almost no understanding of how the American economy operated, wanted no part of any such arrangement. He would rely on noneconomists who shared his political philosophy to formulate the economic policy of the nation.

The chief architects of Reagan economic policy in the early years of the administration were Treasury Secretary Donald Regan and Budget director David Stockman. Mr. Regan, who was the former head of the Merrill Lynch stock brokerage firm, had business experience, but he was not an economist. Many people who are quite successful at business have very little understanding of how the national economy operates. Budget Director Stockman, who was probably the chief architect of economic policy in the early days, had absolutely no formal training in economics. Yet despite the warnings of many outside prominent economists—including recipients of the Nobel Prize in economics—as well as his own hand-picked Harvard economist, Martin Feldstein, President Reagan allowed noneconomists to formulate national economic policy.

Similar actions in other sectors of our economy would be a crime. Suppose a person who had never attended medical school performed major surgery on a patient. What would happen to such a person? He would probably be sentenced to serve time in prison because of the threat he posed to this single individual. Yet people without training in economics were allowed to perform radical surgery on a national economy that affected the lives of nearly 240 million Americans. The damage done to the economy by these people will be felt for a long time to come.

Goals of the Reagan Revolution
In order to understand why a president would ignore the advice of most professional economists and allow noneconomists to formulate economic policy, one must un-

derstand that the goals of the Reagan Revolution were more political than economic in nature. President Reagan came to Washington determined to reverse the political direction that this nation had been following for 40 years. The new President had hated the growth in government social programs that had evolved over the previous 40 years, and he was determined to move the nation in a new direction.

Reagan wanted to reduce the size of the federal government and the role it played in the American economy. He was determined to reduce spending on social programs and increase spending on national defense. And he was determined to reduce taxes, especially for the very wealthy. When supply-side advocates approached him with the Kemp-Roth tax cut proposal and promised that it would lead to a stronger economy, as well as accomplish his political objectives, the President couldn't have been happier.

From that time on, mainstream economists and mainstream economic policies would play little role in the Reagan administration. If the economic advice was not compatible with the goals of the Reagan Revolution, it was to be ignored. In other words, the President was far more interested in accomplishing his political goals than he was in pursuing sound economic policies.

In early January of 1981, Budget Director, David Stockman, who was 34 years old and lacked any formal training in economics, began to formulate plans for the first Reagan budget. When Stockman and his staff fed the data of the proposed Reagan economic program into a computer that was programmed as a model of the nation's economic behavior and instructed the computer to estimate the impact of Reagan's program on the federal budget he was shocked. The computer predicted that if the President went ahead with his promised three-year tax reduction and his increase in defense spending, the Reagan Administration would be faced with a series of federal budget deficits without precedent. The projections ranged from an $82 billion deficit in

1982 to $116 billion in 1984—the year the President had promised to balance the budget. Stockman knew that if those were the numbers included in President Reagan's first budget message the following month, the financial markets would be panicked and Congress would be unlikely to approve the budget.

The young Stockman, untrained in economics, decided that the assumptions programmed into the computer by earlier economists were not correct. So he and his team discarded orthodox premises of how the economy would behave and reprogrammed the computer with new assumptions that would give them the projected balanced budget that the President had promised for 1984. However, later when the nonpartisan Congressional Budget Office projected continuing large budget deficits instead of a balanced budget by 1984, there seemed to be a problem of credibility with either Stockman's numbers or those of the Congressional Budget Office. When President Reagan was asked by reporters why the two sets of projections were so different, he charged that the Congressional Budget Office and members of Congress endorsing the CBO projections were trying to shoot down his economic program by using "phony" figures.

Phony figures were indeed being used, but not by the Congressional Budget Office. Of course, the Congress and the public had no way of knowing at the time that Stockman had rigged the computer at the Office of Management and Budget (OMB) in order to show a projected balanced budget for 1984. It was not until the publication of the infamous article, "The Education of David Stockman" by William Greider in the December 1981 issue of *The Atlantic Monthly* that the public learned the whole story.

Much was learned about the early days of the Reagan Administration from that article which almost cost Stockman his job. When Stockman's appointment as budget director first seemed likely, he had agreed to meet with William Greider, an assistant managing editor at the *Washington Post*, from time to time and relate, off the record, his private account of the great political struggle ahead. The particulars of these conversations were not to be reported until later, after the President's program had been approved by Congress. Stockman and Greider met for regular conversations over breakfast for eight months, and these conversations provided the basis for Greider's article in *The Atlantic Monthly*.

The article became a political bombshell when it was published. In addition to the revelation of the computer rigging in order to get budget projections that could be sold to the Congress, Stockman asserted that the supply-side theory was not a new economic theory at all but just new language and argument for the doctrine of the old Republican orthodoxy known as "trickle down" economics. Basically, this doctrine holds that the government should give tax cuts to the top brackets; the wealthiest individuals and the largest enterprises, and let the good effects "trickle down" through the economy to reach everyone else. According to Stockman, when one stripped away the new rhetoric emphasizing across-the-board cuts, the supply-side theory was really new clothes for the unpopular doctrine of the old Republican orthodoxy. Stockman said, "It's kind of hard to sell 'trickle down,' so the supply-side formula was the only way to get a tax policy that was really 'trickle down.' Supply-side is 'trickle down' theory."

Stockman said that the Kemp-Roth tax cut bill was a Trojan horse to bring down the top rate. "The hard part of the supply-side tax cut is dropping the top rate from 73 to 50 percent—the rest of it is a secondary matter," Stockman said. "The original argument was that the top bracket was too high, and that's having the most devastating effect on the economy. Then, the general argument was that, in order to make this palatable as a political matter, you had to bring down all brackets. But, I mean, Kemp-Roth was always a Trojan horse to bring down the top rate."

Many people were misled by the 25 percent cut in personal income tax rates that was enacted during the first year of the Reagan Presidency. Many thought it meant a 25 percent cut in the amount of taxes each individual paid. But this wasn't true. People who were in the 70 percent bracket, which was cut to 50 percent, saved $20 on each $100 of taxable income. However, a person who was in the 16 percent bracket would have his or her tax rate cut from 16 percent to 12 percent, and would save only $4 on each $100 of taxable income. In other words, the tax cut benefited the rich to a much greater extent than the poor. In fact, because of the substantial cuts in programs that benefited primarily the poor, most poor people were actually hurt by the tax cut.

Studies have shown that persons with an income of $10,000 just about broke even. In other words, any benefits from the tax cuts were offset by losses resulting from cutbacks in government programs that benefited them. People with incomes below $10,000 were worse off after the tax cut, and people with incomes above $10,000 benefited from the tax cut. The higher one's income, the greater the benefit from the tax cut. For example, a person with a taxable income of $500,000 would pay $100,000 less in taxes as a result of the tax cut.

Aside from the effects of the tax cut on the economy, many social scientists believe that the benefits gained by the rich caused undue hardships on the poor. For example, in an effort to save money on the social security program without cutting benefits to the masses, the administration launched a review of recipients receiving social security disability benefits and decided in many cases that the people were not severely enough disabled to warrant continued disability benefits. Thus, at a time when the economy was plunging into a severe recession and many able-bodied workers were unable to find jobs, many people who had become dependent upon social security disability payments as their only means of support suddenly had their benefits cut off   The issue was brought to the public's attention when a man in Pennsylvania went down to the local Social Security office with a shotgun and committed suicide in front of Social Security workers. When police went to the man's house they found a note on the kitchen table that read, "They're playing God. They've taken away my Social Security benefits." Eventually, Congress intervened and brought a halt to the cut off of disability benefits.

Many programs designed to help the poor were cut or eliminated in an effort to afford the big tax cut, much of which went to the very rich. Whether this is right or wrong involves value judgments. However, many Americans who like to think of this country as a fair and compassionate nation feel there was little evidence of concern for the problems of the poor in the Reagan economic program.

The Reagan Economic Record
As President Reagan ended his term of office he claimed that his administration had been one of prosperity. However, the record shows otherwise.

Unemployment
President Reagan had the worst unemployment record of any modern president.   During his first four-year term, the average annual unemployment rate was 8.6 percent—7.6 percent in 1981, 9.7 percent in 1982, 9.6 percent in 1983, and 7.5 percent in 1984. At no other time since the Great Depression of the 1930s had the unemployment rate ever been as high as 8.6 percent even for a single year, let alone for a 4-year average.   If we look at Mr. Reagan's full 8-year Presidency, the average annual unemployment rate is 7.5 percent. Since the Great Depression, only in 1975 and 1976, during the Ford Presidency, has the unemployment rate been as high, in even a single year, as Reagan's 8-year average unemployment rate.

President Reagan tried to blame the high unemployment of the early years of his term on former President

Jimmy Carter. He claimed the economy was already in a recession when he took office. This is not true. President Carter added 10 million jobs to the economy during his four years in office. The unemployment rate was 7.7 percent during the last year of the Ford Administration. During the Carter Presidency, the unemployment rate was reduced to 5.8 percent in 1979 before the economy entered a mild recession in January of 1980 which began driving unemployment back up. However, United States Commerce Department statistics clearly show that the Carter recession hit bottom two months later in March 1980, and the economy began to expand again. The economy was expanding and unemployment was falling when President Reagan took office. However, the economy was very fragile, having just come out of a recession, and it was extremely important that the proper economic policies be followed to prevent the economy from slipping into a new recession.

The policies of the Reagan administration played a major role in the severe recession. The President called upon the Federal Reserve System to pursue a tight-money policy, he cut domestic spending, and he failed to implement his promised first-year 10 percent cut in tax rates that was to have been retroactive to January 1, 1981. The fragile economy could not withstand such policies. Budget Director, David Stockman, who had begun to worry about forthcoming deficits, convinced the President to reduce his first-year tax cut from 10 percent to 5 percent and delay its implementation until October 1.

Thus, instead of the 10 percent cut in tax rates for the entire year that had been planned, there was a cut of only 5 percent, and it was in effect for only the last 3 months of the year. This translates into a 1.25 percent average tax cut for the entire year instead of the planned 10 percent cut. This, combined with the tight money policy and the cuts in domestic spending, was more than the fragile economy could stand. It plunged the economy into the worst recession since the Great Depression of the 1930s, causing millions of Americans to lose their jobs.

The severe recession of 1981-82 did not have to happen. It was caused by government policies. If the President had implemented the planned 10 percent tax cut in January and called on the Fed to pursue an easier-money policy, it is my belief that there would not have been a recession and all the suffering that accompanied it. Of course, the economy could not have withstood the planned two additional 10 percent cuts in the two succeeding years without problems of deficits and inflation. But the first year's planned 10 percent tax cut was very much needed at the time to stimulate the economy.

Inflation

President Reagan claimed that he brought inflation under control. However, Reagan could not take credit for reducing inflation unless he was willing to accept the blame for the recession. The inflation rate came down for two reasons. First and foremost, there is no surer way to reduce inflation than to throw the economy into a severe recession. With aggregate demand falling, it is difficult for prices to rise. As more and more people become unemployed and lose their spending power, sellers are forced to reduce their prices, or at least stop raising them, in order to make sales.

Secondly, much of the inflation of the 1970s was caused by soaring energy prices. The price of crude oil rose from $3 a barrel to $33 a barrel during the period 1973 to 1980. This caused an increase in the price of almost everything because energy makes up a part of the production cost and much of the transportation cost of most products. Just as President Reagan took office a glut in world oil supplies developed, making it impossible for crude oil prices to rise further.

Even if prices had remained at a steady level of $33 per barrel, there would have been no further upward pressures on prices resulting from the energy crisis. But prices of crude oil actually dropped substantially during the

Reagan administration, helping to offset price increases of other items and keep the inflation rate low.

Budget Deficits and the National Debt

The national debt doubled from $1 trillion to $2 trillion during the first six years of the Reagan Presidency, and was more than $2.6 trillion when Reagan left office. However, things were to get much worse during the next four years under President Bush.

Some observers had high hopes that Bush would abandon the economic policies of Reagan that had submerged the government so deep into red ink. After all, Bush had referred to Reagan's proposed economic package as "voodoo economics" during the 1980 primary campaign. It was understandable that Bush would have to support Reagan's polices while he was Reagan's vice president, but once he was elected to his own term as president, Bush was free to take a different course.

But Bush did not change course. He continued to follow the politically popular, but economically disastrous, policies that had already done so much damage to the financial condition of the government. During Bush's four years as president, the on-budget deficit (excluding social security) averaged more than $286 billion per year! And when Bush left office, the national debt that had been only $1 trillion dollars at the beginning of the Reagan-Bush administration, had soared above the $4 trillion mark.

In summary, before the introduction of Reaganomics, the nation had accumulated approximately $1 trillion in national debt throughout our entire history. Twelve years later, the debt had quadrupled. The voodoo economics of the Reagan-Bush years will have a negative impact for generations to come. We can't change that, but we can certainly insist that from now on national economic policies should be based on sound economic principles that are supported by the majority of mainstream economists.

CHAPTER 8

WILL WE BLOW IT AGAIN?

The American economy is once again in one of its best positions ever in terms of its potential to provide long-term prosperity for the nation if the proper economic policies are pursued. But the financial condition of the federal government is, in some ways, the worst that it has ever been. Our economy has been good to us. Our political leaders have not.

The performance of the economy has a direct impact on the status of government finances, yielding abundant revenue in times of full employment and insufficient revenue when unemployment rises. Likewise, government fiscal policy has a direct impact on the performance of the economy, and policy makers have the power to either help or harm the economy.

The proper functioning of the economy is so crucial to the future of our nation and to each and every one of us that common sense would dictate that we handle the economy with kid gloves. Just as the first rule of medicine is to do no harm, the top priority of economic policy should be to avoid any government actions that will harm the economy.

A Review of the Financial Facts

Historians will probably have great difficulty explaining how politicians from both parties were able to portray a government financial status that was as sour as a lemon as one sweeter than honey during the 2000 presidential election campaign. From a historical perspective, the overall financial status of the government is clearly worse than it has ever been. The problem is that the American people, and most journalists, do not know that this is the case. Instead of going to the library or going to the web to find out the true picture, they watch patiently as the politicians add layer after layer of white lace to the façade, making the red ink behind the lace almost invisible.

Budget Deficits and the National Debt

Some people confuse budget deficits with the national debt. A budget deficit is the amount by which expenditures exceed receipts in a single year. The national debt is the total amount that the government currently owes from all of its past borrowing. Any and all money borrowed to finance budget deficits is added to the national debt.

The government has a budget deficit in any year in which its on-budget expenditures exceed its on-budget receipts. No matter how much surplus there may be in the Social Security fund for that year, if the government spends more than it collects in taxes for general government operations, it has a deficit, and that deficit will add to the national debt. No matter whether the government borrows the money from the public or from the Social Security Trust Fund, the national debt goes up, and interest must be paid on the borrowed money.

As of September 30, 1999, the federal government owed $5,606.1 billion ($5.6 trillion.) of which $4,611.3 billion ($4.6 trillion) was borrowed between September 30, 1981 and September 30, 1999. In other words, more than 82 percent of the current gigantic national debt was borrowed during the administrations of President Reagan, President Bush and President Clinton! No wonder President Clinton, Vice President Gore, and Governor Bush want to cover up this ugly picture with layer after layer of lace.

During the Reagan years, the average on-budget deficit was $185.4 billion per year, and the deficit during his last year in office was $194.0 billion. The average annual on-budget deficit during President Bush's four years was $286.3 billion, and the deficit in his last year was $340.5 billion. The Clinton-Gore administration had an average on-budget deficit of $156.1 billion during the first seven years. There was a tiny surplus of $0.7 billion in year seven, and there will probably be a small surplus for fiscal year 2000.

Perhaps Americans have become so conditioned to living with large deficits and a mammoth national debt during the past three administrations that they think of them as normal and don't realize just how uncharacteristic and damaging they are. The five-fold increase in the national debt during the past 20 years is the direct result of the irresponsible large tax cuts during the Reagan years, and America will continue to pay a high price for this unforgivable practice of voodoo economics for decades to come. America should have learned a powerful lesson from the adverse effects of Reaganomics on the American economy. Instead, the nation seems almost anxious to take another lethal dose of unwarranted tax cuts.

Table 8-1 shows the average annual deficits and the size of the national debt during the terms of all presidents serving after World War II. The dramatic increase in the size of the deficits and the growth in the national debt during the Reagan-Bush years are absolutely shocking. How could we as a nation allow our economy and our finances to be so abused by people who weren't even trained in economics?

TABLE 8-1: AVERAGE ON-BUDGET DEFICITS FOR PRESIDENTS SERVING AFTER WORLD WAR II AND SIZE OF THE NATIONAL DEBT AT THE END OF THEIR TERM IN OFFICE IN BILLIONS OF DOLLARS.

President	Years Served	Average On-Budget Deficit	National Debt, Last Year in Office
Truman	1945-53	7.1	266.0
Eisenhower	1953-61	3.1	292.6
Kennedy	1961-63	4.6	310.3
Johnson	1963-69	10.3	365.8
Nixon	1969-74	14.2	483.9
Ford	1974-77	62.9	643.6
Carter	1977-81	54.0	994.8
Reagan	1981-89	185.4	2,868.0
Bush	1989-93	286.3	4,351.4
Clinton*	1993-01	156.1	5,606.1

* Based on 1993-00
Source: Economic Report of the President, 2000

President Truman's term included the last year of World War II and the Korean War. Yet, his average annual on-budget deficit was only $7.1 billion, and the national debt was $266.0 billion when he left office. President Eisenhower had an average annual on-budget deficit of only $3.1 billion during his eight-year term of office. Kennedy, Johnson, and Nixon had reasonably small average annual deficits despite the fact that they served during the Vietnam War. Presidents Ford and Carter did have abnormally high deficits because of the high unemployment during the years in which they served, but even their deficits were small compared to the deficits of our last three presidents.

The Power of Deception

Abraham Lincoln once said, "You can fool all of the people some of the time, and you can fool some of the people all of the time, but you can't fool all of the people all of the time." I think it depends partly on whether or not the people want to be fooled. It seems that for the past 20 years most of the people have been fooled most of the time with regard to government finances by three different presidents. Furthermore, most of the people are currently being fooled simultaneously by one sitting president and two presidential candidates.

None of us would entrust our individual health to an accountant or lawyer no matter how brilliant they might be. Nor would we entrust the maintenance and repair of our automobiles to anyone except highly-skilled and well-trained auto technicians. If we are so particular about who does the maintenance and repair on our automobile, why would we not insist that the far-more-complex mechanism called the American economy also be maintained and re-paired at least under the guidance of highly-trained experts?

Even before the Reagan administration had imple-mented any of its voodoo economics, Americans were warned of the dangers inherent in Reagan's proposals. Paul Samuelson, one of the most brilliant economists who ever lived and the first American to receive the coveted Nobel prize in economics, was shouting out warnings from the rooftops. Samuelson, who wrote a regular column for *Newsweek* at the time, had access to a mass audience and he did everything in his power to alert the masses to the inherent danger in Reagan's economic proposals. Below is an excerpt from an article by Samuelson that appeared in the March 2, 1981 issue of *Newsweek.*

> Reagan's program does attempt a radical break with the past. A radical-right crusade is being sold as a solution for an economy allegedly in crisis. There is no such crisis! Our people should join this crusade only if they agree with its phi-losophical conservative merits. They should not be flim-

flammed by implausible promises that programs to restore the
1920s' inequalities will cure the inflation problem.

It was like shouting into the wind for Dr.
Samuelson. Very few Americans cared about what professional economists thought, even Nobel prize-winning
economists. They believed whatever the charismatic
Reagan told them. He had promised that he could deliver a
major tax cut and still balance the budget by 1984. Why
should the people take the word of Samuelson over that of
the President who had just been elected by a landslide?
Never mind that Reagan chose a 34-year-old with no training in economics as the chief architect of his economic policy or that he ignored the advice of his own Council of
Economic Advisers. Surely the President knew what he
was doing.

Although his policies inflicted great damage upon
the American economy and the fiscal status of the federal
government, Reagan continued to insist throughout his
presidency that. "The American economy has never been
healthier or stronger." Instead of acknowledging that
Reaganomics had led to catastrophic deficits and a sky-
rocketing national debt, and taking remedial actions,
Reagan continued to stubbornly insist that his economic
policies were sound despite the abundant evidence to the
contrary. And the most disturbing part of it all is that the
American people continued to believe him.

The "great communicator" seemed capable of
charming the people into believing the economy was strong
and healthy despite enormous evidence to the contrary.
However, when George Bush tried to follow in Reagan's
footsteps, he was unable to convince Americans, who knew
otherwise, that the economy was sound. Although President Bush seemed such a sure bet for re-election that most
of the top contenders for the Democratic nomination chose
not to run, Bill Clinton saw the incumbent president as vul-

nerable because of the state of the economy and the negative effects of Reaganomics.

Clinton effectively convinced the American people
that something must be done about the out-of-control deficits and was able to get a tax increase through Congress
along with other legislation designed to tackle the deficits.
The deficit-reduction efforts made it possible for Alan
Greenspan and other members of the Fed to ease up on
monetary policy, allowing interest rates to fall, and paving
the way for the long economic expansion.

President Clinton has been a willing participant in
leading people to believe in a nonexistent surplus. However, he has proposed using the surplus to pay down the
national debt. Many Clinton haters do not want to give him
credit for anything, including the prosperity in the economy. However, Clinton has worked closely with Federal
Reserve Chairman Alan Greenspan to foster the right envi-
ronment for economic prosperity. I believe that historians
will give joint credit to Bill Clinton and Alan Greenspan for
the current long economic expansion.

Historians will not, however, give Clinton high
marks on honesty. Many of the reasons that historians will
chastise Clinton for his dishonesty are beyond the scope of
this book. However, his misleading statements with regard
to the federal budget are very pertinent to our discussion.
Bill Clinton is the one who first proclaimed the "good
news" about the federal government having excess money.
It was during Clinton's watch that the Social Security Trust
Fund surplus first became large enough to more than offset
the continuing on-budget deficit. It was President Clinton
who announced a $69 billion federal budget surplus in
1998 when there was really a $30 billion on-budget deficit.
It was Clinton who told the American people that the nation
ran a $124.4 billion surplus in 1999 when almost every dol-
lar of it was in the Social Security Trust Fund and was ear-
marked for funding the retirement of the baby boomers.

In a sense, President Clinton was a mentor to both Al Gore and George W. Bush. It was only because of Clinton's proclamations about an alleged surplus that Al Gore and George W. Bush were able to make the alleged surplus a "credible" political issue. And Clinton continued to add fuel to the flames of financial deceit as convention time neared for the two major political parties. On June 26, 2000, President Clinton announced that "over the next decade, the federal budget surplus will total nearly $1.9 trillion." That was more than 2 ½ times what the administration predicted it would be just four months earlier.

This was music to the ears of Governor Bush who proclaimed the projected surplus the "peoples' money" and reiterated his proposal to cut income taxes by $1.3 trillion during the next ten years. But the projections, based on assumptions right out of fantasyland, were as bogus as the alleged current surplus. Even President Clinton acknowledged their uncertainty. "This is just a budget projection." Clinton cautioned. "It would not be prudent to commit every penny of a future surplus that is just a projection and therefore subject to change."

How could anybody put any credibility in a projection process that yielded 2 ½ times as much surplus in June as it had yielded just four months earlier in February? The American public was once again being duped by clever politicians into believing that the government did have surplus money.

When there is an extremely strong desire for some unlikely event or circumstance to be true, people look for any evidence they can find that it is true. And when a sitting President of the United States and the presidential nominees of both major political parties say that it is true, the public accepts it as fact. Such is the case of the alleged budget surplus.

To date, the only on-budget surplus is the $0.7 billion reported for 1999. Thus, during the past 20 years, the government has borrowed more than $4.6 trillion ($4,600 billion) to cover its deficit spending. The only offset to this red ink spending is the tiny $0.7 billion on-budget surplus reported for 1999.

There was a surplus in the Social Security Trust Fund of $123.7 billion for 1999, and the Trust Fund is expected to continue to run sizeable surpluses over the next 10 years until the baby boomers begin to retire in 2010. However, this surplus exists by design. The increase in Social Security taxes resulting from the 1983 legislation to prepare the Social Security system for the big financial hit that it will take when the baby boomers retire is not general revenue. Every penny of the Social Security surplus will be needed to fund the retirement of the baby boomers.

Federal law mandates that Social Security funds be kept separate from general revenue. Congress would never have passed, and the American people would not have supported, the 1983 increase in Social Security taxes if they had thought the revenue would later be used for general government funding. Indeed, Senator Moynihan advocated repealing the increase when President Bush used the funds for general government and to mask the true size of the deficit. It is the ultimate in deception for the government to add the $123.7 billion Social Security surplus to the meager $0.7 billion "real" (on-budget) surplus and publicly announce an official surplus of $124.4 billion!

The Power of Education

The only way to battle the deliberate deception of American voters with regard to both the economy and the status of government finances is education. Sound economic policies that will enable the American economy to function properly are absolutely crucial to the future of the nation and to all of its citizens. We dare not allow our economy to be used as a political pawn by politicians who are more interested in getting elected than in pursuing sound economic policies.

We must provide economic education to the young people of this country as well as to adults who have never received such education. It is crucial that Americans have enough knowledge of basic economics to distinguish between sound economic-policy-proposals and voodoo economics. Voters must know enough basic economics to enable them to avoid being misled by clever politicians.

Our young people are exposed to American history and civics lessons in the lower grades. They are taught these same subjects in both junior high and high school. It is education for citizenship, but there is a gigantic gap in that education because of the lack of instruction in economics. The field of economics is so broad that there is almost no aspect of our lives that does not involve economics.

Economics is one of six fields in which the coveted Nobel prize is awarded to "persons who have made outstanding contributions for the benefit of mankind." Yet the vast majority of American children go through the entire K-12 series of studies without ever being exposed to economics at any level. Furthermore, the majority of college graduates have never had a course in economics. As a result, only a tiny fraction of the American people have any notion of what the subject is about, although economics has a more direct effect on their lives than any other subject.

This is crazy! How could the most advanced nation in the world have allowed such a critical gap in its education system to go unfilled for so long? Why are schools not now rushing to add economics to their curriculum?

Education is a powerful instrument in any society, and the addition of economics to the curriculum of most schools in this country could eventually have an enormous impact on the economic policies of our government. If the majority of Americans knew just a little about economics, voodoo economics could become a thing of the past. The American people would not support economic policies that were not in the best interest of the nation, and they would reject politicians who proposed such policies.

Planting Safeguards for the Future

The American people are at a great disadvantage in trying to determine which economic proposals are correct and which ones are not. We need some objective way of separating the politics from the economics. It would help so much if we had someone we could trust to blow the whistle on politicians who are trying to deceive the public with regard to economic policy.

Below is an excerpt from the July 31, 1990 *CONGRESSIONAL RECORD*, page E2561. It is the reading by Congressman Terry L. Bruce of Illinois, of a proposal for a mechanism to protect the public from continued voodoo economics which I had written in my weekly newspaper column on the economy in 1990.

ECONOMIC ADVISORY COUNCIL

_____

HON. TERRY L. BRUCE
OF ILLINOIS
IN THE HOUSE OF REPRESENTATIVES
Tuesday July 31, 1990

Mr. BRUCE: Mr. Speaker, Dr. Allen Smith of Eastern Illinois University in Charleston, IL, has written an excellent column proposing a national economic advisory council. I ask that it be put in the CONGRESSIONAL RECORD, and I urge my colleagues to give it careful consideration. His message is something all of us should ponder.

UNDERSTANDING ECONOMICS No. 28
(By Allen Smith)

THE NEED FOR A NATIONAL ECONOMIC
ADVISORY COUNCIL

In an effort to get the economy out of its current mess and prevent economic malpractice in the future, I propose the creation of a nonpartisan national economic advisory council made up of nine of the best economists in

America. The council members, who would serve nine-year staggered terms, would be appointed by the President and confirmed by Congress.

Council members would be ineligible for reappointment so they could remain independent of partisan politics. Since it is essential that council members have a strong grasp of basic economics, only professionally trained economists would be eligible to serve on the council. The council would have only advisory powers, but it would be mandated by law to issue periodic public reports on the state of the economy and on economic policy.

The purpose of such a council would be to serve as a watchdog for the American people to ensure that sound economic policies are followed. Sound economic policy is not Republican, Democratic, conservative, or liberal policy. It is policy based on basic economic principles which are supported by the majority of professionally trained economists. Like members of any other profession, economists disagree on certain aspects of economic policy, however, there are many fundamental principles of economics upon which most economists agree. It is some of these most basic fundamental principles that have been ignored in recent years.

This proposal will be about as popular with most politicians as a bad toothache. But if enough Americans supported such a proposal it could be enacted into law. Since members of the council would be appointed, and ineligible for reappointment, they could put the interest of the economy and the American people ahead of any partisan political goals. They would be free to openly disagree with the President and Congress, and they would be obligated to report economic malpractice to the public.

Since the council would have only advisory powers, it could not prevent all economic malpractice or ensure sound economic policy at all times. But, since it would be free to criticize government economic policies without fear of reprisals, it would tend to force the government to pursue responsible economic policies. It would also ensure that professional economists have advisory input into national economic policy.

The actual structure and functioning of any such economic advisory council could differ substantially from my proposal. The important thing is that the American people need a group of highly competent economists who are

looking out for the public interest instead of the interests of
partisan politicians. Such a council would also benefit the
many government officials who have had little or no formal
training in the subject of economics. These officials cannot
formulate sound economic policies without the advice of
competent economists.

Since members of the President's Council of Economic Advisers are selected on the basis of their compatibil-
ity with the President's political goals, they serve the political interests of the President which are not always compatible with sound economic policies. The American people
need a council of nonpartisan competent professional
economists who are mandated by law to promote economic
policies that will best serve the long-term interests of the
American economy and the American people.

I have already met privately with a member of the
U.S. Congress to discuss the feasibility of creating such a
council. He is testing reaction to the proposal in Washington, and he may draft a bill proposing legislation that would
create such a council. Enacting such legislation will require
massive support from the general public. Politicians will not
take the initiative in creating a council that would serve as a
watchdog for the American people to ensure that politicians
put the interests of the American economy above their own
political interests. Such legislation will be possible only if
the American people demand it. If you support the creation
of a nonpartisan national economic advisory council, please
send copies of this column, along with your letters of support, to your elected representatives Washington. We must
do more than talk about the need for sound economic policies. We must take action to ensure that they become a reality. Our future, and the future of our children and grandchil-
dren, is at stake.

I am even more convinced today than I was ten
years ago that the American people need some kind of independent committee or council of competent economists
to monitor economic policies and blow the whistle on politicians who put personal political interests above the interests of the economy and the American people. The specific
provisions of the proposal that I submitted to Congressman
Bruce ten years ago could be altered in various ways and

still serve the same purpose. The important thing is to have competent economists monitoring economic policies and reporting economic malpractice to the public at large.

If Abraham Lincoln were president today, there might not be a need for such a watchdog council. We might be able to count on him to be truthful with the voters and to pursue only policies that were in the best interest of the nation. But it has been a long time since we have had a president who could even come close to filling Lincoln's shoes in terms of honesty and integrity.

Presidents who have made it to the White House, not by ambition, but by a willingness to answer their country's call to service, have put the good of the nation and the American people at the top of their priority list. Neither George Washington nor General Dwight D. Eisenhower wanted to be president. Both resisted early efforts to get them to consider running. But they both finally answered the call to serve their country one more time. Neither of these men "needed" to be president to feed their ego. Their willingness to accept the position was motivated by their patriotism and their desire to be of service to their country.

Unfortunately, few modern American presidents or presidential candidates have been so motivated. So, just as other modern-day employers must be vigilant in monitoring their employees as a deterrent to misbehavior, we citizens must monitor our employees, including the President of the United States, to make sure they do not betray our trust.

A Personal Plea

I'm not sure whether or not this is ever done in books, and I'm not at all sure how readers will react to it. But I am going to conclude this book with a personal plea to the American people to please check out the facts and stand up for America by standing up for economic literacy and sound government economic policies.

Given the response to Paul Samuelson's pleas twenty years ago, this effort would seem doomed to fail from the very beginning. If a giant among economists such as Paul Samuelson could not wake up the American people, then the chances of an ordinary college professor doing so are probably about as good as the chances of an ice cube surviving a whole day in the blistering summer sun. But I must try.

Partisan politics and selfish political agendas have gotten out of hand in this country, and they threaten the very fiber that holds America together. Our two-party system has failed us during the past two decades. Although there are still minor differences between the two parties, they have moved so close together that there doesn't seem to be a very significant difference between them anymore.

Most of the candidates seem to be more motivated by personal ambitions and a desire to keep the political contributions flowing in than they are by any burning obsession to do what is best for America and its people.

It has taken me a long time to reach this painful conclusion. I grew up on an Indiana farm with parents who were so honest that they would cheat themselves in order to be absolutely sure that they didn't cheat others. As a small child, I believed that everyone was honest. I thought that honesty was just an innate part of being an American, and I held government leaders in especially high esteem. The stories I learned about Abraham Lincoln and George Washington in elementary school led me to think that all presidents were cut from the same material. I even had a secret ambition to someday run for Congress as a way of serving my country.

A college education cleared up a lot of my misconceptions, and it was while I was still in college that I realized I would never want to run for Congress or any other political office. It became clear to me that there is a lot more potential for making a significant positive contribution to society outside of government than there is inside government. So I decided to become a college economics professor in the hope that I would at least have a little impact on society through the thousands of students I would teach throughout my career.

But I'm no longer sure that I, or my colleagues in the field, have had very much of an impact on the thinking of Americans. It has been devastating for me to observe the needless suffering that has taken place over the past twenty years because of economic malpractice. It was like watching a child needlessly suffer the consequences of a horrible illness for which a cure was available. And it is especially painful for me to see how easy it is for politicians to pull the wool over the eyes of the public today because of the widespread economic illiteracy.

This book represents my best chance to make a difference in reducing economic illiteracy and in promoting sound economic policies. I have no idea how many people will read the book and, of those who do read it, I can't be sure that a single person will be persuaded to stand up for America by standing up for economic literacy and sound government economic policies. But I am hoping that, if I choose my words carefully and say just the right things, I just might have a slim chance to make a difference.

I am not asking much of readers or the American people. I am only asking that you check out the facts and try to stimulate public debate on the economy and on the financial status of our government. However, I do have a special challenge for members of the news media, especially those who have direct contact with the candidates. Dig out the facts and report them to America. If two newspaper reporters could bring down a powerful American president by just going after the truth and reporting it, then this assignment should be a piece of cake.

Instead of just reporting what the candidates say about the economy and the budget, interview competent economists and accountants. Check the figures on government finance that are available to all citizens. The truth about the economy and the federal budget is not hard to find. It is available from the web sites of the Treasury Department, the Office of Management and Budget, and many other sources. Please check out the facts and report them to the American people.

For those reporters who are so fortunate as to have direct access to the candidates, I have a special challenge. Ask the candidates tough questions about the economy and government finance. Challenge them to make public their credentials for managing the economy, including how much formal training they have had in the field of economics. Ask them why they think that a nation that has run an on-budget deficit in 38 of the past 39 years is suddenly going to begin having huge annual budget surpluses over the next decade. Ask them how they can justify using the funds that Americans have contributed to Social Security for increased general government spending or for giving tax cuts to the rich.

American journalists have the power of a massive army when it comes to battling ignorance, misinformation, and outright deceit. If they keep the heat on the candidates and check out the accuracy of the candidates' public statements, the American people will benefit enormously.

This book will become available to the public approximately six weeks before the fall election. But there is still time to battle the irresponsible proposals of both candidates and try to get them to pledge that their economic policies will be based on sound economic principles.

The answer to the question, "Will we blow it again?" will be determined by the American people. The future of America is in our hands. If we push hard for educating the public in the field of economics, and if we demand some kind of watchdog mechanism that will deter officials from engaging in voodoo economics, history will record the presidential election of 2000 as the time when the American people finally responded to decades of economic malpractice by saying, "NO MORE VOODOO ECONOMICS!"

INDEX